So You Want T
Teacher'

MW01133211

by Jim Wilhelm
(The Community College Experience: Teaching from the Inside)

Introduction-Never in my wildest dreams!

The goal of this book is to provide guidance to those of you who are interested in teaching at a community college, or even teaching in general. Please know that this is not your run-of-the-mill book on academic constructs and progressive paradigms for community colleges. It is, however, a pragmatic guide with some scholarly references and actual experiences you may find useful. Thinking back on my career, there were many times I could have used some advice on what I was doing when I began teaching, and I trust this book will clarify some expectations for you to assist you in making an informed decision when choosing your career in teaching. I discuss many scenarios you may encounter in an attempt to better prepare you for what is ahead. Teaching is certainly an honorable profession and I would not trade this career for any other. There are rewards way beyond money awaiting you! At the end of the book I have a survey for you to take to gauge your propensity for teaching in the community college arena. You may find it helpful as you are deciding on a career path. I give you insights into my experience and mix pep talks with humor. While I enjoy humor, please know that I take teaching/learning very seriously. We are training students to become better thinkers, deciders, and citizens. I still remember my mother telling me that an education is something no one can ever take away from you. They might steal your money or material possessions but your education is forever. When you improve your mind, you improve your life. My parents taught me well and I hope this book orients you into a brilliant career of service that you will always cherish.

Never in my wildest dreams had I considered a teaching career. I was an insurance adjuster for General Motors and was on special assignment for two years training dealers on the West coast about a new computerized claims reporting procedure. I traveled to different sales territories in California, Washington, and later, New Mexico, where the local salesperson had already set up training meetings of from 10 to 50 people. After one particular session a saleswoman, Nell, who became my good friend, asked me if I had ever considered teaching. I laughed and dismissed the offer. She persisted and told me that every time someone asked a question my eyes lit up and I always answered with a helpful, enthusiastic response. I thanked her for the compliment and did not give it much thought. A year later, when I returned home from my special assignment, I remembered Nell's compliment and had a chance to teach a night class at the local military base teaching Principles of Management. I still remember being petrified in front of eight students, but after a couple of class meetings things began to flow more naturally for me. I thoroughly enjoyed the experience and six months later applied to be a Business instructor at our local community college (South Plains College). I was later told there were seven finalists and most had more teaching experience, but they took a chance on me. I will always be grateful to Nell for her keen observation and compliment. Thanks, Nell!

My first semester with the college, the department chair asked if I liked my job and I told her that I loved it. I was a bit puzzled as to why she would ask such a question, but she said she was concerned because I seldom left my office and did not socialize much with colleagues. I told her I was simply preparing for classes and wanted to stay ahead of the students. I tend to over prepare and over achieve, but it was important that I do so in this case. After my first semester, I relaxed some and started socializing more with colleagues. A brief note here: As in any job field, please give yourself a fair chance to work into teaching, it is different and certainly not a 9-to-5 job, so it may take a couple of semesters before you feel comfortable; but on the flipside, you should know for certain after two semesters if this is the job for you. I believe there is nothing worse than a teacher who does not want to be here but hangs on for, say, stability or a paycheck. It is a waste of everyone's time and you could be out finding another career that you would enjoy.

This semester I completed my 25th year at the community college and I have cherished the students, the opportunity for personal growth, the freedom to basically control my own future, and the overall experience in general. I plan to teach until it is no longer fun, or they run me off, whichever comes first!

I start my discussion with the purpose of the community college and its place among other institutions. Next, I will compare the community college to proprietary schools and discuss how teaching is different from other professions. The challenge of open admissions and teaching developmental classes will also be covered. Then we will look at faculty, students, promotions and motivation. I also explore the "call to teach," technology in teaching, and teaching style. Finally, I will regale you with my own experiences and some stories that will paint a more complete picture of this profession. Please note you will also find a self-survey in the Appendix to help gauge your propensity and enthusiasm for teaching in a community college. So, let's get started!

About the Author

Jim D. Wilhelm has a B.B.A. in Business Administration, an M.S. in Management, and an Ed.D. in Higher Education/ Administration from Texas Tech University. He is currently a Professor of Business Administration at South Plains College, Lubbock, Tx, which is 30 miles from the main campus in Levelland, Tx. His background includes working for General Motors as an insurance adjuster for 13 years, with his last two years spent as a trainer.

Wilhelm has taught courses for AT&T and Southwestern Public Service Co. He is certified to teach Speech and has taught, or is teaching: Principles of Management, Principles of Marketing, Small Business Management, Supervision, Human Relations, Introduction to Business, Personnel Management (now Human Resources Management), Business and Professional Speech, and Developmental Math. He has been with the college for 25 years, advises Business majors, and has sponsored Phi Beta Lambda (business society) and Phi Theta Kappa (honors society).

TABLE OF CONTENTS

Motivating Students
How Do You View Your Students?
A Balancing Act
Summary

CHAPTER 1

PURPOSE OF THE COMMUNITY COLLEGE

Minor institutions just a few decades ago, community colleges are now a major player in American society. A generation ago, public two-year colleges were called junior colleges, were considered unimportant, and enrolled only a small portion of college students. Now called community colleges, they have become comprehensive institutions that have greatly increased in size and importance, and serve a broad segment of the community. Where enrollment in four-year colleges has doubled since 1965, enrollment in community colleges has increased five-fold. Today, almost half of all new college students are in community colleges (NCES, 2002). The community college has historically been the link between high school and college. In 2004, there were 1158 community colleges in the U.S. (Phillippe & Sullivan, 2005, p. 9)

The Need for Community Colleges

Community colleges are amazing institutions designed around an idealistic goal: increasing college access. Community colleges are the primary source of opportunity for ethnic minorities, immigrants, and low-income students. They offer a second chance for students who attended poor high schools, or who did poorly in high school. Besides preparing students to transfer to four-year colleges, they also offer certificates and associate's degrees in occupational fields (Brint & Karabel, 1989), as well as a wide range of noncredit classes, training activities and community services (Rosenbaum, Deil-Amen, & Person, 2006).

Post-World War II, traditional four-year universities were criticized for being unable to meet the needs of a changing economy and society. The U.S. community college, in part, evolved as a "feeder" institution to provide educational opportunities for students (a) who did not fit the "traditional" profile, (b) who lacked a sufficient academic background for entrance to four-year universities, or (c) who could not afford university tuition. The resulting community college countered the notion of higher education as a venture intended for only the few. Contemporary U.S. community colleges are publicly supported institutions that are accredited to award the associate degree as the highest degree. These institutions combine introductory-level academic transfer programs, adult basic educational programs, remedial education, vocational/technical educational programs, and community services (Cohen & Brawer, 1996).

Recent projections issued by the National Center for Education Statistics call for 7.5 million students to be enrolled in community colleges by 2016--an increase of almost 14 percent over the 6.5 million students enrolled in 2005 (National Center for Educational Statistics, 2007).

Brief History

The community college began as part of a plan to break undergraduate degrees in half—the first two years broad and general, the third and fourth years aimed at immersion in the perspective and methods of a discipline (Deiner, 1986). In their early history, two-year colleges expanded with the purpose of serving as vehicles for providing local access to the freshman and sophomore years of bachelor's degrees, but as community colleges evolved their orientation toward the baccalaureate changed. Community colleges developed multi-faceted missions. In addition to university transfer, they added remedial courses, vocational training, and classes of interest to non-degree seeking students (Blocker, Plummer, & Richardson, 1965). Here in the twenty-first century, the community college remains comprehensive, but priorities shifted. At present, job training overshadows other aspects of the school's mission or purpose (Ayers, 2005).

In 1995, Smith wrote a scathing review of our educational system and the need for higher education in the book *Tomorrow's Community College*, of which I agree, in it he says:

> *The break-up of the traditional family and the rise of families with two wage-earners has often produced parents who are more concerned about earning money than rearing and educating their children. Leave education to the schools and to the educators has been the refrain of some parents. But schools cannot provide an adequate education for most children without intensive, extensive and continuing support from parents. This is not happening in*

today's America and it is not likely to happen in tomorrow's America. And we have not yet invented a viable substitute.

The efforts to educate our children in America have been greatly hampered by television an industry hungry for ratings and dollars no matter what the cost to society. Television has attracted millions of our young people to sit far too many hours in front of a screen watching programs with too much violence and sex, creating a world of unreality for young people. TV has taken our young people away from relaxing and studying and homework; away from play and wholesome games and exercise; away from employment and away from parental influence and caring.

Just as damaging is the failure of our educational system to impart to our students often enough an understanding and appreciation for democracy. We have a citizenry today that is often politically illiterate, often uncaring about and essentially uninterested in the political process. This caused to some degree by television programming that has failed in its responsibility to inform and arouse the public sufficiently to participate in the political enterprise. Democracy cannot long exist without well-informed, active participants who make rational decisions based on what is best for the entire society. The combination of an inadequate school system and an uncaring television industry has been devastating to the development of responsible citizenry. They are often unprepared to vote intelligently, and are easily subjected to special interests or often do not care much about the entire enterprise. So few citizens vote today that most decisions are being made by a small minority of the total society.

The American school system is not only a failure for many young people as individuals, but it is the primary reason for many national problems. A good example is the "welfare problem." Anyone who has been close to this issue knows it is to a major degree an educational problem. Too many "dependent children" drop out of high school—often because of unwanted pregnancies—and become enmeshed within the welfare system from which they have great difficulty leaving because they are unprepared for gainful employment or for further education. Another example is our "crime problem"—a problem that often involves young people who are disenchanted by the school system and elect a career of crime rather than one of employment. Meanwhile, business and industry have been forced to spend millions of dollars each year to educate their employees, because the school system failed to do so adequately.

There's no doubt that the breakdown of our American moral fiber has contributed greatly to current societal dilemmas. With half of marriages ending in divorce, television and computers taking the place of actual face-to-face conversations, and American complacency at an all-time high is it any wonder that we need to prioritize our values? There is no magic solution but I do know that education plays an important role in bettering our lives. The community college continues to elevate individuals into solid, hard-working citizens.

Challenges Aplenty

The challenge for the community college is to balance learning standards with open enrollment policy. Open enrollment policy benefits students who do not qualify for enrollment in a traditional university due to reasons such as low entry-exam scores or students who have limited financial resources. In the U.S., tuition and fees are substantially less than those of four-year public or private institutions. Universities can set a certain score level for a student to be admitted, whereas the community college welcomes everyone because this is our mission. However, this can be a double-edged sword because while we are giving access to a greater number of students, we must strive to keep learning standards high so that, if students choose to, they may continue on to a university or simply get a solid education by obtaining an associate's degree.

If I had it to do over, I would have chosen to start my higher education at a community college because of less expense for the same quality. I would have had smaller classes and probably would have enhanced my education, rather than sitting in monster classes for Economics, Finance, Psychology, History, and Government. The monster classes weren't particularly difficult because we could not participate, due to time constraints. I sat with 200-300 other students and took notes from lectures. Then I regurgitated the information back on exam day. When I reached my junior year I had been conditioned by the security blanket of the monster classes and not having to participate. However, suddenly I was in class with only 12-15 students and I HAD to participate! It is quite a transition because now you must take part in discussions and give your opinion. This is simply another difference between community colleges and universities. I don't know if one delivery method is better than the other. And, in defense of universities, they must have monster classes because of state budget cuts and trying to provide education to the masses. I have many students who are apprehensive about moving on to a huge university campus after experiencing the smaller community college atmosphere. I always tell them they'll be fine and have a small circle of friends like anywhere, but, in actuality, I was petrified my first few days at a university. I remember standing at the center of campus with a map and determining where all of my classes met. It was a scary, but rewarding process because I was maturing as an individual. It is a ritual most students complete successfully.

Community colleges are caught in the vortex of a revolution as profound as that which brought them into the postsecondary education scene. It is a customer revolution, a service revolution, a learning revolution, a digital revolution, an information revolution, an industry revolution, and most significantly, a revolution in organizational dynamics. Learners are coming from every direction--from companies and K-12 schools, from regional communities and nations throughout the world, and from socioeconomic backgrounds ranging from affluence to poverty. These learners have expectations and needs, and they expect colleges to respond to them--not once, but again, and again, and again. Their needs include convenience; reasonable cost; state-of-the-art technology; courses anytime, anywhere, anyplace; service on demand; amenities like close-in parking and food service; learning that is relevant to life and a career; and outcomes that meet or exceed personal goals (Alfred et al., 2009, pp.3-4).

The mission of the community college is to provide (a) open access to education; (b) comprehensive educational programming; (c) service to the community; (d) teaching and learning; (e) lifelong learning; and (f) student success. These institutions are to be commended for their efforts in: (a) enrolling nearly half of all undergraduate students in higher education; (b) creating opportunities for underrepresented populations, which traditionally have not had access to higher education; (c) preparing a skilled workforce by enhancing employment skills and certifying students in various fields (e.g., health, technical fields); and (d) providing a platform for students to transfer into a four-year university (Nevarez & Wood, 2010).

The community college I am employed by has basically two curricula areas: academic and technical. The academic side includes courses such as: English, Math, Psychology, History, Government, and so on. The technical side includes programs that augment core courses such as: Business, Office Technology, Automotive Technology, Medical Transcription, and so on. The technical courses are in specific skill areas to assist the student in acquiring employable skills. Since I teach Business courses, my discussion in this book will be from the technical side of the community college.

Although community colleges are a major segment of U.S. higher education, they are typically dismissed as institutions of the last resort. Community colleges play an increasingly important role in providing advanced educational opportunities for a growing number of students. Especially now at the beginning of the twenty-first century, when state appropriations to community colleges are being cut--forcing community colleges to dramatically raise tuition and fees to compensate for these cutbacks (Levinson, 2005, p.1).

In a world where workforce development has become the primary mandate for all higher education institutions, community colleges will continue to stand in the vanguard. Their ability to rapidly design and implement curriculums for emerging career fields has always given them a competitive edge over other education providers. For that reason, courses in fields such as bioterrorism, complementary health services and nanotechnology can all be found at community colleges today. The colleges can be expected to continue this rapid curricular response in the future as societal and technological developments lead to the creation of career fields unimagined today (Phillippe & Sullivan, 2005, p. 161).

Summary

In summary, the history of the community college involves providing the opportunity for higher education for people who somehow don't fit the traditional university student mold. There is a great need for community colleges. Many countries allow only their elite to attend college, but the United States gives everyone an opportunity to go to college and excel. With all of our faults, our nation still allows anyone with determination and motivation to avail themselves of a higher education. Education is essential to becoming a productive, intelligent citizen, and the community college fills this role well!

CHAPTER 2

THE COMMUNITY COLLEGE VS. PROPRIETARY SCHOOLS AND ACCREDITATION

Once upon a time, the competition facing community colleges was confined to the educational arena: colleges, universities, and each other. In the 1990's, competitors from outside of education worked hard to compete with traditional higher education providers. Corporations, temporary agencies, and for-profit organizations competed for students and for their share of the higher education dollar in many states (Alfred & Carter, 1996).

Community Colleges vs. Proprietary Schools

It is important to note that community colleges differ extensively from the proprietary, for-profit institutions that flourished after World War II. Whereas those institutions were largely created to teach a relatively narrow skill, community colleges, especially those that call themselves "comprehensive," are more involved in providing some modicum of the general education typically included in many of the higher education institutions (Levinson, 2005).

A proprietary school, on the other hand, is owned by someone or an entity. So, naturally, the school's objective is to make a profit or they must close their doors. Many times they have their own governing board so one must be careful about faculty credentials. It may be a good outlet to getting a quick certificate or degree (many offer 6 month to 1 year programs) depending on the subject matter or specific skill acquired. The key to deciding whether a community college or proprietary school is best relies with the employer. After all, the goal is to get a job and if the degree is accepted by that particular employer, then that degree is acceptable.

The two primary types of for-profit colleges are enterprise institutions and multicampus corporations. Enterprise institutions are usually locally or family-owned, are relatively small, and have a very informal structure and operating style. By contrast, multicampus corporations result from either modular development or purchase of smaller independent colleges. They generally have relatively large enrollment on each campus and typically offer some online degree programs. The largest of these corporate colleges, in terms of number of campuses and number of students, are the Apollo Group (primarily University of Phoenix), Corinthian Colleges, Career Education Corporation, Education Management Corporation, DeVry University, Kaplan Higher Education, Strayer Education, and Sylvan Learning Systems.

For-profit colleges have successfully attracted students because they offer degrees in curricula that are in high demand from employers and students (especially applied business, computer science, and technology), promote hands-on learning, have a customer service orientation, offer courses at convenient times, operate year round, and emphasize career placement. These institutions have very low unit costs of operation because of economies of scale, no frills but modern physical plants and equipment, and typically contingent and part-time faculty. The market potential for-profit college activity is largest where employer demand for new employees or continuing professional development is high and public college offerings are few or nonexistent (Floyd, 2007).

In 2013, another proprietary school prepared to enter the local competition but as of this writing it has yet to open its doors. It was to offer associate's, bachelor's, and master's degrees in Lubbock, Tx (Lubbock Avalanche-Journal, 2012). Their associate's degree, a 24-month program in business, would cost the student approximately $37,000 in tuition and fees, according to their website. In contrast, at South Plains College, the school I'm employed by, the same 24-month associate's degree in business will cost the student approximately $7,500 in tuition and fees. Do I need to state my case further for going to a community college?

Relatively few full-time faculty members are employed at for-profit institutions, and tenure is virtually nonexistent. "Faculty governance," a much-discussed issue among traditional institutions, is not even a topic, let alone an issue, among for-profits. Semesters, quarters, or academic terms in large part have given way to courses that begin and end based on the completion of core course requirements or the passing of a competency exam. Students have a wide array of options for when they begin and complete courses. The institutions still provide traditional seat-time programs leading to degrees, but the fastest growing segment of higher education is online programming with certificate-based as well as degree-based coursework that has been powered by for-profit and corporate universities. Students generally are admitted the day they apply or make their enrollment deposit. The age of the student is irrelevant. For-profits are also more diverse than most traditional institutions; half of their students are minorities, half are women, all age groups are represented, and there is a mixture of full- and part-time constituencies. Students are as likely to take courses in an office building or in cyberspace as they are on a campus. Accreditation remains important, especially as eligibility for student loan funds depends on it. But accreditation is not essential for every institution and may be more associated with national occupational specialties than with regional efforts. For-profits have questioned the importance of accreditation and have suggested an alternative means of organizational certification that would be attached to program specializations rather than geographic regions of the country (Tierney & Hentschke, 2007).

Proprietary, or for-profit, schools generally will pay lower faculty salaries because of the aforementioned bottom line. They are in it to make a profit! Judging by flooding the airwaves 24 hours-a-day with advertisements about their particular school, they are apparently, very profitable institutions. However, please beware, I just saw a news report on television the other day about proprietary schools being investigated because of high student loan default rates and the fact that students were promised jobs that simply did not exist. The big caution here is to do your homework. Always research and compare institutions, and as I said earlier, if your job will accept credits from such a school then go for it.

Advantage: Community Colleges

It is obvious that I am biased towards the community college because I teach here. This is not an indictment of proprietary schools and the deciding factor should be what the student needs to learn, how quickly, and if they can find employment with that degree or certification no matter where it is from.

Conversations with currently enrolled students and recent leavers indicate that community colleges have successfully differentiated themselves from other institutions by employing practices that place students at the center of everything they do.

They accomplish this by reaching out through instructors and staff to gain insight into what students want and need. Community colleges offer convenience in all forms and have earned a reputation for learner-centeredness by constantly searching for new and novel ways to meet or exceed student needs. Advantage will reside with those institutions that strive to provide better service to the constantly changing needs of learners. Beyond convenience, there are other ways in which community colleges exceed the performance of rivals in meeting learner needs. Consider the following:

> *Smaller classes taught by instructors who are focused on teaching and learning.
> *One-stop facilities which provide integrated services to students at entry.
> *Cooperative programs with K-12 schools (dual enrollment, assessment, etc.) and employers that ease the path to attendance.
> *Instructor sensitivity to variable learning styles and the need for varied instructional modalities.
> *Easy-entry/easy-exit procedures for students.
> *A focus on delivering value through service in contrast to making service available (Alfred et al, 2009, p. 8).

There are some big differences between high school, community college, and university teaching. My sister, Jody, taught in the public school system for over 30 years and I admire her greatly! In fact, I admire anyone who teaches in the public schools. I remember hearing nightmare stories from her about having to grade papers the entire weekend or being on call so that parents could call teachers at home. She had to buy a lot of her own school supplies (I made several bookcases for her classroom). My friend, Susan, teaches computer technology in high school. She said she usually has two preps but has had as many as five. She has been teaching for 30 years and says that discipline is a factor. Discipline is very time-consuming because between tending to students needs and them acting up in the classroom, it detracts from teaching/learning. I would not be an effective public school teacher because, to me, I would have to spend too much time on behavior problems. Maybe that's a reflection of my own schooling. I always felt sorry for the substitute teacher because we would put them to the test. It is a fact of life that at that age the student is learning boundaries and what they can and cannot get away with. That is the nature of the game. I carry my share of guilt for some of the things we high schoolers put our teachers through. I had many fine teachers and am sure they had the patience of Job and the determination of a marathoner to even show up for class some days. High school teachers go into the profession with eyes wide open, knowing the challenges they will face. This is why I admire them so much, and they deserve lots of appreciation for shaping young minds with knowledge and patience. High school teachers are heroes on any measurement scale!

Teaching at the university level one generally is required to have a doctorate, but there is also the pressure of publishing 2-3 research articles annually plus the normal teaching load. Of course, research precedes good teaching but I wonder when the focus shifts from teaching to publishing if the student pays the price. It seems more universities are hiring professors who do nothing but research, or rotate researching one year and teaching the next. That is a good approach to building your research base and still funneling up-to-date information into the classroom.

I chose the community college so I could focus on teaching and not have pressures of publishing (the University), or discipline problems likely to detract from learning in the classroom (the public schools). The downside to teaching only, is losing sight of research studies and upgrading skills. Sometimes we get too comfortable and teach the same thing over and over and over. Again, if I do that, I am cheating the student. Being a community college teacher entails lots of self-discipline. If I chose to, I could teach, keep my office hours, and then go home every day (I have seen many do that). But don't I owe it to the students to be accessible, keep my office door open, volunteer to sponsor a club, and constantly be alert to new learning opportunities for the classroom? You bet! If you don't commit to being the best teacher you can be, then find another career. This is not a part-time job to supplement your income while you do some other job (yes, I know instructors who look at it that way also). Make a full-time commitment to your teaching because the rewards will be phenomenal!

Finally, the concern for accountability represents the wider change in the complex relationship between higher education and society. Higher education no longer simply resides in society; it is of society, increasingly subject to society's prevailing ideologies, ways of viewing the world, its transitions and upheavals. Higher education no longer simply shapes society through its knowledge contributions; it is rather shaped by society through the knowledge specification – both in terms of students and research – which the latter contracts with higher education to deliver (Light, 2000).

Accreditation

In order to ensure a basic level of quality, the practice of accreditation arose in the United States as a means of conducting nongovernmental peer evaluation of educational institutions and programs. The community college is accredited by, in our case, the Southern Association of Colleges and Schools (SACS). It is the governing body to oversee such things as qualified faculty, appropriate facilities, degree/certificate offerings, and basically everything pertinent to making sure the student is receiving a quality, up-to-date education. SACS has six regional accreditation organizations recognized by the U.S. Department of Education. So it follows that the community college is a state-supported, nonprofit educational facility. Accreditation by the Southern Association of Colleges and Schools facilitates the transfer of credit to other colleges and universities.

Many colleagues, including myself, do not look forward to all of the paperwork and time involved in showing accountability for everything we teach. After all, we've already done this for years, but it has previously occurred behind the scenes, or individually in class. Now, we must justify each course and each program's existence to show relevance. It is tedious, to say the least, but isn't it necessary to show accountability? This is a meaningful transition to prove that we are teaching skills needed in life and in the workplace. Whether the accountability movement was precipitated by state budget cuts or consumers wanting value for their buck doesn't matter. What does matter is improving student's lives.

Community colleges receive most of their funding from federal, state, and local taxes, with by far the greatest support coming from state and local tax sources. On average nationally, community colleges receive approximately 39 percent of their funds from state taxes, 18 percent from local government, 20 percent from tuition and fees, 13 percent from the federal government, and 10 percent from other sources. As is true with so much else about community colleges, funding is characterized by its diversity and varies from state to state and, in some cases from college to college within a state. While some community colleges receive large portions of their budgets from local sources, others receive little or no local tax support (Vaughn, 2000). In 2007-2008, my institution, South Plains College, received funding from the following sources: student and parent, 41.4%; state, 35.5%; and local, 17.4%. In 2012, our college received only 34% of funding from state taxes which was down from the 35.5% in 2007-2008. Since the state of Texas deregulated college tuition, funding from the state has been reduced systematically each year for colleges and universities. This reduced funding forces higher education institutions to raise tuition rates dramatically in order to meet budget shortfalls.

"Why do community colleges work?" President Clinton asked. "Well first of all, they're not encumbered by old-fashioned bureaucracies. By and large, they are highly entrepreneurial. They are highly flexible. They are really democratic—small 'd'—they're open to everybody. And people work together. And when something doesn't work they go do something else." (Smith, 1995).

Summary

In summary, as I mentioned, the advantages of attending a community college include the stringent accreditation the school goes through to insure a quality higher education, plus the cost of enrollment is much less than proprietary schools. Again, proprietary schools will have shorter programs at higher prices and for the individual who needs quick training a proprietary school may be the answer. The community college fulfills community needs for quality higher education.

CHAPTER 3

LIKE NO OTHER PROFESSION

What are the basic expectations of your job, with regard to teaching?

1. You arrive on time and prepared for each class session.
2. You have a clear, understandable speaking voice.
3. You dress professionally, within the expectations of your campus culture.
4. You teach the curriculum, not your personal opinions and worldviews on any topic.
5. You have office hours and meet with students as needed.
6. You respond to students' emails and calls in a timely manner.
7. You don't have a lot of student complaints.
8. You are open and receptive to having your classes observed formally and informally by colleagues and supervisors.
9. You grade papers in a timely manner.
10. Your grading is fair and based on established criteria.
11. You cover the appropriate amount of material for each course (Clement, 2010).

<u>You Are Always Teaching</u>

Many people, including some of my friends, think that teaching is an easy job because once you teach the course you can just repeat the lecture over and over. In many ways, I probably thought the same thing when I started. Nothing could be further from the truth, because as a teacher I have class on my mind 24 hours-a-day. My friend, Susan, (the high school computer teacher) works 45 hours a week, but that is only physical classroom time. Many hours outside the classroom are spent in preparation. I mentioned earlier that this is not a 9 to 5 job. You may need to teach mornings and evenings some days. I sometimes miss, but not very often, the 9 to 5 routine where I could check in and out daily and seldom have to take work home. It was a matter of divorcing my mind from work and having my own life after 5 p.m. A teacher never completely turns his or her mind off because they are always looking for new information tools or techniques to better reach students. I am continually reading the paper, researching, and listening to trends that I can bring into the classroom for relevance. If you cannot relate subject matter from the world for the student, then interest wanes. The challenge comes when teacher motivation wanes and the temptation is to fall into a stale routine with nothing new to offer. After all, if you have tenure you have basic job security. But please DO NOT take that route! Teachers are, in effect, actors on a stage and we must keep the audience listening and involved or they will want their money refunded because the show was lousy. When I fall asleep during my own lecture I know it is time to change things up. I am a big fan of The Wall Street Journal. The Journal gives great, up-to-date information on marketing and management news as well as financial data. I also watch local news and read the local newspaper so that I can apply business concepts to everyday life. This helps excite students and keeps them motivated when they see immediate application of business principles. And, of course, the textbook is invaluable as the course guide.

I love teaching, but not so much the administrative duties. I think most teachers prefer teaching rather than attending meetings, working on budgets, and so on. I know I do. At this point, we need to discuss the "recruiting" aspect of the job. You will be expected to represent your program or major field of study at community job fairs or any events that involve community interface with the college. This has been a subject of debate among faculty members because there are two sides to this. On the one hand, faculty feel that counselors/recruiters should bear the brunt of these events because that is in their job description. On the other hand, the counselors/recruiters simply remind us that if our program is not represented at an event then we cannot complain about not having enough students to make a class. Personally, I try to attend all events that don't conflict with class time.

Expectations

While doing my research, I came across an interesting book from 1970, *Teaching in the Community Junior College*, by Kelley & Wilbur that listed "Ten Commandments" for successful community college teaching. It seems after more than 40 years, expectations have not changed much. Here is the list:

1. *You must desire and enjoy teaching.* There are hundreds if not thousands of different occupations and professions in our society. Are you positive that teaching is what you want to do through most of your life? Practice teaching should help to provide an answer. If you use teaching merely as a fill-in or stepping stone to *some other* profession, the chances are that you will not be the most effective teacher--or a happy one.

2. *You must prefer teaching a variety of adults, young and old.* Students at these levels are distinctly different. If you teach at the collegiate level when your interests and aptitudes lie in another level, you may be an unhappy and ineffective teacher.

3. *You must be sold on the values and contributions of community college education to society.* If you teach in a community college without being convinced that it is serving a worthwhile purpose in education and that it should have as much respect and value as any other type of college, you may be discontented and ineffective.

4. *You must like a community college atmosphere of academic work and life.* Local community colleges have very close identification with specific communities and therefore generally create a different atmosphere from one surrounding four-year colleges and universities. Local two-year colleges are as much a part of communities as are local elementary and secondary schools. Within the academic work and life in the community college, you should find a suitable academic climate.

5. *You must be reasonably satisfied with the maximum salaries and benefits you can obtain at the two-year college level.* Some teaching benefits are shared by teachers at all levels of education, but some others relate only to the community college. You cannot

make your maximum contribution without being reasonably satisfied with what the community college can offer to you personally.

6. *You must be dedicated to your task.* You are dedicated if you utilize all of your energies and enthusiasm in the job that must be done. Fulfilling the five previous commandments does not automatically imply that you have this dedication. Here we are talking about total commitment and vital drive and motivation. We are talking about inspiration and eagerness, resourcefulness and industry.

7. *You must be vitally concerned about the growth and development of your students.* Your task is to take your students down the educational path toward certain goals. Your aim must be to help these people obtain some measure of success as they traverse this path and to enhance their growth and development by fostering in them the pride of self-accomplishment. No other aim in teaching can be as significant.

8. *You must strive to become an excellent teacher, one who knows and uses effective methods and techniques.* Fostering positive growth and development depends, in part, upon desirable teaching procedures. Classroom procedures and policies will vary even among excellent teachers, but there is a general standard conducive to the best climate for learning. Your methods must relate to two realities of community college teaching: its transfer courses are restricted to the lower division; its student body may include many who are neither highly motivated nor academically strong.

9. *You must know your subject matter and students and express positive attitudes toward both.* If methods and techniques are half of teaching skill, then subject matter mastery and knowledge of students are the other half. Mastery of subject matter should develop with teaching experience, and the teacher must continually learn from this experience in order to

improve his mastery. Your ultimate success also depends upon the degree of enthusiastic, optimistic feelings you have toward both your discipline and your students.

10. *You must have other personal attributes that make you a genuine, empathetic human being.* You may not be the kind of person who is denied a teaching certificate on grounds listed in various state education codes, but you might be a rather unhappy person. According to Pullias, you can be no better as a teacher than you are as a person (1963).

Though needed personal traits may be extensive, generally you must be a well-adjusted, socially acceptable person, and with your students you need to be *fair, friendly, and firm.*

It's Called Customer Service For a Reason

Like it or not, we are in the customer service industry. Organizations are increasingly oriented toward service to clients, patients, and customers. We live in a service economy where relationships are often more important than products. Restaurants, hospitals, banks, public utilities, colleges, airlines, and retail stores all must now gain and retain the patronage of their clients and customers. In any service-type firm, there are thousands of "moments of truth"—those critical incidents in which customers come into contact with the organization and form their impressions of its quality and service (Reece, Brandt, & Howie, 2011).

I remember being hired and how proud I was to be a "college instructor." It boosted my self-esteem and I took my responsibilities very seriously. The customer service aspect has to do with how we treat our customers (students). If we give lousy, rude service, then chances are students may not sign up for our classes. That, in turn, affects the reputation of not only the department but also generalizes to the college itself. You may need to teach several morning and night classes. People ask me why I would want such a schedule and I simply answer that that's the best way to recruit students. Sure, I don't have a life most days but it is up to us (faculty) to flex, not our customers (students). I would love to teach only day classes but such a schedule would adversely impact professionals who cannot attend day classes. Some instructors lose sight of that fact. Maybe it's human nature to take the easy route? I don't know. But if you are not committed to teaching students at times that are best for THEM to attend, then find another career. Okay, I'll step away from the podium for now.

Community colleges serve historically disadvantaged groups: women, minorities, people of low socio-economic status, and first generation college students (Adelman, 2005). As professionals, our challenge is to provide those students with an education of the same nature and character that one finds at the top levels of our postsecondary network. To offer community college students anything less is to partake in a subtle, but socially consequential form of bigotry. Unfortunately, when we limit the scope of our efforts to simply training employees, we deny our students the broad education for citizenship that takes place at the upper levels of the postsecondary hierarchy (Hanson, 2010).

I mentioned SACS (accrediting body) earlier and there is also the State Coordinating Board that must be satisfied. The call for greater transparency and accountability in higher education with respect to student learning and institutional effectiveness is not a fad. The pressure to demonstrate in real and concrete ways that students are learning, and that institutional resources are effectively and efficiently marshaled in support of teaching and learning, is at the heart of future governmental and popular support for higher education.

Rather than hope that accountability is yet one more movement blazing across the higher education horizon toward oblivion (remember zero-based budgeting and total quality management?), the move toward greater accountability and transparency should be embraced by colleges and universities as the basis for more effective communication with both internal and external constituencies (Middaugh, 2007).

We are constantly updating catalog course descriptions, working on class schedules for upcoming semesters, doing annual budgets, typing up goal statements, not to mention attending committee meetings, and so on. Teaching is like no other profession and you will definitely stay busy and challenged.

Summary

In summary, community college teaching is like no other job. You will always be teaching and learning regardless of whether or not you're in a classroom. Expectations for yourself and your students should be high. The "Ten Commandments" for successful college teaching seem rather strict, but those commandments remind us of our huge responsibility to students. It will most likely be the most challenging, yet rewarding career field you could choose. Teaching transitions nicely into customer service because that defines the interaction with students. Treat your customers (students) well, and they are likely to return, which means they will learn not only in your class, but also continue learning for a lifetime.

CHAPTER 4

WHAT IS A DEGREE?

Each year, students come to American college and university campuses to embark on a new journey in their lives. For most, it is an opportunity to acquire the knowledge and skills necessary to pursue careers in their chosen fields. For some, it is an experience encompassing much more than just acquiring knowledge and skills. For others, higher education is a life-changing event. Regardless, most students' primary purpose is to prepare for some form of life's work (Scott, 2010).

A degree is a ritual process where you complete courses and attain a goal. A degree tells the world that you are employable and trainable. Whether a student completes a certificate or degree, it is a measure of accomplishment for that student. It shows the student has proven at least the following: ability, discipline, time management skills, maturity, dedication, determination, and learning ability. A college graduate demonstrates to the employer that he/she can achieve and has built a foundation of knowledge that sets them apart from someone who only completed high school. The person is motivated to accomplish and that's huge for an employer. In some cases, students decide to, for example, major in chemistry in high school, major in chemistry in college, and later become chemists. That is great if you can decide early in life what you want as a career. However, many of us do not have pinpoint focus to major in a particular field and continue with that career for life. Almost anyone you ask knows someone who is working a different job than their major in college, that's okay. This proves that a college degree shows that a person has a certain level of maturity and is trainable. Without college, we would be working many jobs to gain experience and may never learn what we truly should do for our life's work. You would, therefore, have to work several jobs before deciding what you wanted to do with your life. Whereas, college accelerates your life experiences and opportunities because it exposes you to various subjects within a matter of a few semesters or years that helps direct you towards a career. For instance, a student might take an accounting course and discover they would like to major in accounting. The college experience also makes for a better educated citizen. College graduates have access to more information which in turn helps them make better choices. In a nutshell, college is a no lose proposition and broadens your horizons!

A Degree Serves a Purpose

One of the community college's primary purposes has been to accept students from secondary school, provide them with general education and introductory collegiate studies, and send them on to senior institutions for the baccalaureate. An associate degree usually qualifies the recipient to enter the university as a junior. However, certain courses may not be acceptable, some university departments may require alternate courses, and transfer may not guarantee entry to the particular program a student desires.

Career programs are established with the intention of serving students by preparing them for employment and serving industries by supplying them with trained workers. The college staff presumably initiates programs by perusing employment trends in the local area and surveying employers. Program coordinators are appointed and advisory committees composed of trade and employer representatives established. Funds are often secured through priorities established by state and federal agencies. The entire process suggests rational program planning. Nonetheless, questions have been raised about the appropriateness of certain programs and whether the matriculants are well served, and much research on program effects has been conducted.

Most students in vocational programs seem satisfied with the training they receive. Follow-up studies routinely find 80 to 90 percent of the program graduates saying that they were helped and that they would recommend the program to others. Among the students who do not complete the program, a sizable number usually indicate that they dropped out because they received all the training they needed in the courses they took, not because they were dissatisfied with the program. Employers seem satisfied as well. Respondents to surveys of businesses and industries give high marks to community college-based training programs (Cohen & Brawer, 2003).

Growing and Maturing

College accelerates maturity also. The student learns time management skills; such as, when to study for what class. They typically juggle 2-5 classes and possibly a job, so multi-tasking is a must. In addition, they may be rushing a fraternity/sorority so this also plays into the mix.

In undergraduate school, I had a friend who was always on the dean's list in engineering and one day we were playing tennis. It was a very competitive match and we were playing a third set to determine the winner. We were tied 4-4 and suddenly Steve stopped and said, "it's 4 o'clock, I need to go study." I pleaded with him to finish the match and he started gathering his things instead. He said we could finish the match next time we played. Although I was upset, he taught me a great deal that day. I quickly learned why Steve was on the dean's list. He had the self-discipline to succeed.

If you ever lived in a dorm, it was a great maturing opportunity. We all learned to do laundry and budget our money. For instance, I figured out in one load of laundry not to wash a red sweater with light-colored clothes. We clipped discount coupons for meals and generally learned how to pool our efforts for efficiency. I knew when I could nap between classes and when I had to study. The dorm was usually noisy in the evenings so I adjusted more study time to afternoons, or frequented the library in the evening. It seems silly now, but it took me a couple of semesters before I would go to the library alone. I usually would go with a buddy or two and we would meet back at book check-out at a predetermined time. That was simply part of my maturing process. A professor once told me that the library is a great forever friend and he was right. When I focused on the task at hand I had no problem going alone. Looking back, it was not the fear factor of having to go to the library alone but rather the socializing with friends to and from the library that I looked forward to.

The benefits of a college degree are numerous, individuals benefit themselves and their communities as follows:

1. *Socially*. Social benefits include: (a) increased local, state, and federal tax base through annual earnings; (b) increased diversity in the workforce; (c) independence from social services that lead to

draining tax revenue and reductions of programs in a variety of social service areas.

2. *Politically.* Political and civic benefits include: (a) increased likelihood of civic engagement (e.g., voting, community service, engagement); and (b) representation in influential political positions (e.g., federal, state, local boards, commissions, and committees).

3. *Economically.* Economic benefits include: (a) increased earning potential and subsequently philanthropic donations; (b) increased likeliness of job satisfaction, attainment, and security. As a result, students make more money to better support themselves, their families, and communities.

4. *Psychosocially.* Psychosocial benefits include: (a) increased adaptability to workforce needs; (b) increased likelihood of solidified social and professional networks; and (c) increased likelihood of being diversity minded, as a result of increased interactions with individuals from other cultures.

5. *Cognitively.* Cognitive benefits include: (a) increased likelihood of becoming a critical consumer; (b) increased job skills (e.g., writing, reading, communication); and (c) increased adaptability to learning (e.g., professional, social settings) (Nevarez & Wood, 2010).

Degree Statistics

The U.S. Census Bureau (2008) reported the percentage of the U.S. population by highest degree earned. They noted that approximately 65.9 percent of the U.S. population possesses a high school diploma, 30.9 percent for whom this was their highest degree. Thirty-five percent hold at least a two- or four-year degree (8.2 percent and 17.8 percent for whom the associate or bachelor's degree were the highest degree earned). Of these, approximately 9 percent hold at least a master's or professional degree (6.6 percent and 1.3 percent for whom the masters' or professional degrees were the highest earned). Of the entire population, only 1.1 percent have earned doctoral degrees.

Stated more simply, if there were a 100 total high school graduates, 35 would graduate from college with at least an associate's degree, nine would achieve master's or professional degrees, and one would receive a doctorate.

What is an education worth? Education matters. On average students earning an associate degree have salaries 20 to 30 percent higher than individuals who only completed high school. Students who earned a bachelor's degree resulted in significant returns between 56 and 66 percent more than high school graduates (Bailey, Kienzl, & Marcotte, 2004). The emphasis in the United States on knowledge acquisition has contributed to a growing wage gap between high school and college graduates.

Community college programs have been able to prepare much of the mid-skilled workforce in the United States, which includes over three-fourths of first responders (firefighters, police officers, and emergency technicians) as well as half of health care technicians and nurses. Two-year colleges are the fastest growing sector in American higher education (Schmid, 2010).

Summary

In summary, is college worth all of the time and money invested? Yes, it's worth it! I have many, many students over the age of 25 (nontraditional students) who have come back to college to finish what they started long ago. Their lives were interrupted by various circumstances (pregnancy, marriage, tragedy, etc.) but eventually they got back to the core values and realizing how valuable a college education is in society today. Many of my favorite students are older; they are focused and oftentimes are the best students in class. I enjoy watching someone "grow" who has been out of school for 20 years or more. They will start with some hesitation and nervousness for the first few weeks, but then they progress rapidly and self-confidence and self-esteem skyrocket as they realize they can compete favorably in college classes. This is simply another reason why I love teaching!

CHAPTER 5

THE CHALLENGE OF OPEN
ADMISSIONS/DEVELOPMENTAL COURSES

Today's professors are faced with the challenge of instructing 18-year-olds who may not share their values or their work ethic; who cannot read, write, speak, or do math proficiently, or who do not know how to behave appropriately. In the same classroom are nontraditional-age students who come to class with different agendas than typical 18- or 19-year-olds. Some are women who have raised their children and are ready to resume a postponed career. Others are single parents who see education as a means of creating better lives for their families. Yet others are middle-aged and older men who have been forced into or have chosen a career change. Many of these adults are unsure of themselves as students but are not afraid to question and challenge. They are investing hard-earned or borrowed dollars in their education and demand a return for their money (Baiocco & DeWaters, 1998).

Need for Remediation

Of all postsecondary educational structures in America, the public community colleges have borne the brunt of the poor preparation of students. When sizable cohorts of well-prepared students were clamoring for higher education, as in the 1950s and early 1960s, the community colleges received a large share of them. But when the college-age group declined and the universities became more competitive for students, the proportion of academically well-prepared students going to community colleges shrank. Thus, the colleges were dealt a multiple blow: relaxed admission requirements and the availability of financial aid at the more prestigious universities, a severe decline in the scholastic abilities of high school graduates, and a greater percentage of applicants who had taken fewer academic courses.

The community colleges responded by accommodating the different types of students without turning anyone away. They have always tended to let everyone in but have then guided students to programs that fit their aspirations and in which they have some chance to succeed. Students who qualified for transfer programs were never a serious problem; they were given courses similar to those they would find in the lower division of the four-year colleges and universities. Technical and occupational aspirants were not a problem, either; career programs were organized for them. Internal selectivity was the norm; failing certain prerequisites, applicants were barred from the health professions and technology programs. The students who wanted a course or two for their own personal interest found them both in the departments of continuing education and in the transfer programs.

The residue, the poorly prepared group of high school pass-throughs, has been the concern. What should the colleges do with marginally literate people who want to be in college but do not know why? How should they deal with someone who aspires to be an attorney but who is reading at the fifth-grade level? (Cohen & Brawer, 1996)

How can students with such poor academic records and experiences acquire confidence that they belong in college? Faculty help students acquire confidence by explaining to students that their poor performance is due to poor high schools. Faculty were acutely aware of students' backgrounds and the difficulties they present. A math professor at Northwest talked about how students who perform poorly often come from "weak educational backgrounds."

> *The students were not raised in either a cultural atmosphere conducive to education, or the school was overcrowded, or there were too many kids in the classroom. They were improperly developed. We meet those needs here too. I have taken students from remedial math all the way through differential equations. This can be done, but it requires historically redoing a lot of things.*

Rather than criticizing students for low achievement and the negative pressures in their outside environments, faculty accepted these factors and incorporated these realities into their teaching strategies. Faculty reported that it is their job to help the student overcome such disadvantages. Students must be given the time, attention, and assistance they need to succeed. Faculty were committed to this idea and saw it as one of the main functions of a community college (Rosenbaum, Deil-Amen, & Person, 2006).

As open admission institutions, community colleges accept all who apply, often resulting in a need to supply heavy remedial needs and a last-minute scramble to accommodate all who enter in a given semester. An immediate challenge is to provide the assessment, advising, and placement services that these students need. Given fifty percent of community college students are first-generation college attendees, there is a great need to help students acclimate to the college experience. Often a student will begin the enrollment process by taking a placement exam that assesses his or her reading, writing, and mathematical abilities. The results of this assessment are then used to place him or her in the proper level of courses in English or mathematics or possibly in courses for adult basic skills or ESL (Levinson, 2005).

Developmental Course Statistics

With approximately forty percent of all college students needing remediation in one or more areas, there is job security in teaching remedial Math, English, or Reading. I find it interesting that several years ago they were called "remedial" courses and that seemed to morph into "developmental" courses and now they are called "learning assistance" or "learning support" courses.

In my research, I did find a difference between "remedial" and "developmental" classes. The "remedial" courses consist of basic reading, elements of English, and basic arithmetic. These courses assume students possess fundamental cognitive deficits in need of remediation. The courses focus on academic content typically covered in middle school or early high school. At most institutions, these courses are a prerequisite before students may enroll in the next course in the academic sequence (Boylan, Bonham, & Bliss, 1994). Exit competencies of remedial courses generally prepare students for subsequent enrollment in a developmental course by teaching the needed skills and knowledge. For example, successful completion of a remedial course in fundamentals of mathematics provides a student with skills needed to enroll in an intermediate algebra course. Few students could complete the fundamentals of mathematics course and have a high chance of success in a college algebra course (Boylan, 2002).

In contrast with "remedial" courses, "developmental" courses focus on students' strengths, develop both cognitive and affective domains, and build skills necessary for success in college-level courses. Remedial courses look to the past and focus on acquiring the skills and knowledge that should have been obtained while in high school; developmental courses look to the future and the skills needed for success in college. Typical developmental courses include intermediate algebra, college textbook reading, learning strategies, and basic writing composition (Arendale, 2010).

I don't see any significant difference between "remedial" and "developmental" courses and it seems to me to be splitting hairs a bit because by any name, remediation of students is a primary function of community colleges and we are trying to teach the student skills that raise them up to "college-level" classes. At my community college, in math, for instance, the student starts with "developmental algebra," then moves to "beginning algebra," then progresses to "intermediate algebra." After having passed the series of three courses, the student is then prepared for college-level math.

The following finding comes from the U.S. Department of Education's study focusing primarily on developmental courses (National Center for Education Statistics, 2003). Of students enrolling in these courses, three-quarters successfully complete them. Most students enroll in developmental courses during only one academic term. Students are twice as likely to enroll in the courses at two-year institutions than in four-year colleges and universities. About three-quarters of institutions offer only institutional credit for the courses, while others offer graduation credit. In these cases, the credit counts as a free elective. About three-quarters of institutions require students to enroll in remedial or developmental courses based on their entry-level test scores (this includes my community college, South Plains College).

Since some of my classes don't always make, I found great solace in adding Developmental Math to my repertoire. It is like nothing I have ever taught before. In my Business classes I sometimes adjust the grade slightly upward due to a student's effort, participation, and attendance. Math is totally different. If the student does not master problems, then they do not move on to the next level. It would be a disservice to that student for me to fudge and put them in the higher level Math where they have little chance of success. It does not matter how much I like the student or how much effort they are exerting, either they can work the problem or they can't. Of course, that's as it should be. It does not make it easy on me when I see a student progressing and trying very hard but their grades are below passing. Most students cheerfully take the course again and succeed but I wonder how many get discouraged and drop out? When the student has to go through all three levels of developmental Math before reaching college level does it discourage, or encourage? That sounds like an excellent dissertation topic/study for someone.

Advising Students

Another challenge that will take plenty of patience on your part is advising students. I recall my college days and being sent to the back of the line when I did not have a form filled out properly. I read the general catalog thoroughly beforehand and knew what courses I needed before seeing my advisor. My advisor required that you do most of the work yourself. Of course, they were there to answer questions but if you were not prepared, to the back of the line you went. Well, when I first started advising students at our community college it was a real eye-opener! They walked in my office without a clue as to what they wanted to take or should be taking. At first, I was amazed that they had no direction whatsoever. It was as if their parents dropped them off at the front door and told them to go enroll in something. Many times you can send them to a general counselor who will be most helpful. But I usually try to assist them by finding out about them and what their interests are before guiding them into my Business program or any program. I have a lot of students who plop down in front of my desk and simply say, "I want to take some classes." So it will be up to you to draw them out and dispel some myths and to educate them in knowing the registration procedures and what courses they need. If you do a good job of advising, your program will always be full of students who graduate with your major.

Along with institutional procedures, instructional activities are also part of the equation in fostering student success. Labor market success does not depend solely on institutional charters and employer links. Students also need subtle soft skills to find, secure, and maintain jobs. Traditional college procedures assume that college students already possess such skills, yet many two-year college students come from disadvantaged backgrounds and often have not been exposed to the behavioral codes and social cues necessary to succeed in the professional world. Besides helping students to catch up academically, colleges can also help many students catch up socially, providing them with direct guidance about how to dress, speak, and interact in job interviews and in the professional workplace. In many cases, if colleges do not provide this soft-skill training, the benefits of the academic education that they offer may be lost in the labor market (Rosenbaum, Deil-Amen, & Person, 2006).

Going back to the mission of the community college, it is generally open admission so that, in itself, presents challenges. It is a fact that some students are not college material and you will have to deal with those types of challenges. But that is another reason I like community colleges because it does give students a chance to prove themselves. How do you know unless you try? I will discuss motivation in a later chapter but I love to see a student learn, blossom, and achieve what they didn't think they could. I see many from, lack of a better term, "negative families," who message their children that they don't need to or aren't smart enough to get a college education. Later on it is a wonderful, gratifying moment to see them walk across the stage and receive their certificate or degree.

Regarding developmental classes, many blame the high school for not preparing the student for college-level work. Of course, it is not that easily explained, because I believe everyone shares the blame to a certain extent (government, state requirements, funding cuts, and so on). This is not a treatise on finding blame. The point is, the student needs some assistance to reach college-level courses. The developmental classes are certainly full every semester which proves there is a definite need.

Summary

In summary, we can discuss colleagues, administration, class workload, or even hours, but by far the biggest challenge will be teaching a mixture of high-level students with those students who need remediation. It's a worthy but trying mission and I relate some stories about that in Chapter 15. You will be frustrated at times because you'll feel that certain students should not be taking college courses. The key is to not judge from your own frame of reference, remember you're dealing with totally different students than when you were attending a university. They all have a right to be in college and they have the right to succeed or fail. There are so many rewards when you see a highly motivated student who may not have the initial skill set work hard for several years to obtain a college degree. That's what keeps me going!

CHAPTER 6

THE CALLING

I had never believed in someone getting "the call" to teach. I had heard many people talk about it but as I age I am beginning to change my tune. If you feel like you have a unique talent to want people to succeed and you enjoy helping others achieve goals then you probably do have a "calling."

I think commitment and passion are the two biggest concepts for teaching well. As in anything, if you are not committed to something then you will not do a very good job. When I taught Speech, students wanted me to just assign them an informative or persuasive topic and I refused. I told them to speak about something that interested them and they would do a much better job than if I assigned topics. I remember doing many assigned research reports in school and dreading it. When I got to choose a topic I was interested in I always got a higher grade. Students, collectively, will attempt to wear you down. Certainly they do not wear you down on purpose but because you have to deal with so many problems all at once, it can be very exasperating. For instance, you are trying to get an exam ready, you are working on budgets or a committee issue, two students want recommendation letters, your colleague is sick and asks you to fill in, and you do not feel very well yourself. If you are not committed, it will certainly show! Passion is, to me, the overwhelming desire you have to do something. Passion, among other definitions, is defined as: "a strong liking or desire for or devotion to some activity, object, or concept." (Webster, 1991). Passion is excitement and enthusiasm about your career. You look forward to the daily challenges and learning how to deal with those feeds into more passion.

The demand to "make something of yourself" through work is one that Americans coming of age hear as often from themselves as from others. It encompasses several different notions of work and how it bears on who we are. In the sense of a "job," work is a way of making money and making a living. It supports a self defined by economic success, security, and all that money can buy. In the sense of a "career," work traces one's progress through life by achievement and advancement in an occupation. It yields a self

defined by a broader sort of success, which takes in social standing
and prestige, and by a sense of expanding power and competency
that renders work itself a source of self-esteem. In the strongest
sense of a "calling," work constitutes a practical ideal of activity and
character that makes a person's work morally inseparable from his or
her life. It subsumes the self into a community of disciplines
practice and sound judgment whose activity has meaning and value
in itself, not just in the output or profit that results from it
(MacIntyre, 1981).

Though the idea of a calling is closely tied to the biblical and
republican strands in our tradition, it has become harder and harder
to understand as our society has become more complex and
utilitarian and expressive individualism more dominant. In the mid-
nineteenth-century small town, it was obvious that the work of each
contributed to the good of all, that work is a moral relationship
between people, not just a source of material or psychic rewards.
But with the coming of large-scale industrial society, it became more
difficult to see work as a contribution to the whole and easier to view
it as a segmental, self-interested activity. But though the idea of
calling has become attenuated and the largely private "job" and
"career" have taken its place, something of the notion of calling
lingers on, not necessarily opposed to, but in addition to, job and
career. In a few economically marginal but symbolically significant
instances, we can still see what a calling is. The ballet dancer,
devoted to an ill-paid art, whose habits and practices, beautiful in
themselves, are handed down in a community based on a still-living
tradition, so the lives of the public may be enriched, is an example.
In any case, however we define work, it is very close to our sense of
self. What we "do" often translates to what we "are" (Bellah, 2008).

In teaching, either you are in or you are out. If you cannot
take time to prepare well and have the patience to put up with some
malarkey, find another profession. Teaching is not for you.
Teaching may be ripe for professional "rambling and opinions,"
more than other careers because you'll have a captive audience.
However, if you are not prepared, sure, you can play a video or have
class discussion. But students are very perceptive and will figure out
quickly that there is no learning taking place and you are not
prepared. I try to cover the book as much as possible because that's
the book I chose and that's where exams will originate. I also

temper the book with lecture, discussion, and an occasional video to help the student learn the concept.

Regarding teaching, I like the way Sandra Balli (2009) said it in talking about relationships:

> *Teachers and students coexist in classrooms of imperfect people with intricate and fragile human natures. This reality presents a considerable challenge for human interaction; teacher to student, student to teacher, and student to student.*
> *The hundreds of encounters among this tangle of people are significant, sometimes pivotal, impacting classroom life and relationships in profound ways. Teachers have long known that classrooms are a breeding ground for an assortment of irritations as well as affirmations, indifferences as well as connections, and misunderstandings as well as harmony. Along the way, human emotions and interactions mingle and merge, often in unpredictable or unintentional ways, but all contribute variously to strong or strained relationships among those who abide together in classrooms.*
> *As the persons responsible for classroom life, teachers hold the key to setting the tone and charting relationships. Understandably, in the daily hum of classroom discourse, teachers often go about the work of schooling unaware that their particular habits--their passing encounters or purposeful interactions—sear remarkable images into the minds of students for good or ill.*

The above statements emphasize the importance of doing your best teaching each and every day and being a good role model. We never know how much of what we say and do in the classroom impacts students' lives so we must continue to strive for excellence in our teaching!

My Experience

I tend to be an overachiever and one thing I love about teaching is not just that it is only for a semester at a time, but that it has a beginning and an end. You get to have at least two fresh starts each year to improve or do things differently if you so choose. I was an insurance claims adjuster in my previous life and I did not realize how frustrating it was until I left that job. No matter how hard I worked, there was no end. The claims just kept coming and many times I felt no sense of motivation or achievement. If I worked my buns off to clear all of my files then they would send me out to help in another territory. I needed the sense of accomplishment and I could not thrive in such an atmosphere, but teaching is totally different. It just feels good to finish one task (the semester) and then prepare for the next one (the next semester). Being a teacher, I mostly have control of my own destiny. I can go back to school to obtain another degree, I can teach an extra course, I can stretch my imagination by trying a new teaching method, or choose a more relevant book. But there is a beginning and an end to each semester so I can feel a sense of accomplishment. It is almost like running a marathon. You keep running and running, get into a rhythm and suddenly you are at the finish line after months of training. Was it worth it? You bet! I love the semester system because it is a constant source of renewal. So if you get "the calling" consider yourself lucky, but if you don't then that is okay, too.

In graduate school I took a class entitled "Philosophy of Education," and our semester assignment was to define a "good teacher." I was lucky enough to research Quintilian (1969), an ancient Greek sophist upon whose research much of our modern day educational system is built. He defined his 'ideal' teacher, this way: "the teacher should be pure in character, adopt a parental attitude, be strict but not austere, be ready to answer questions, praise recitations of pupils equally, he must avoid sarcasm and above all abuse." Two thousand years ago he espoused the virtues of flexibility in teaching and matching teaching style to learning style. That is difficult to do in college over a 16 week period, but I try to be flexible by varying lectures with videos and group discussion. My exams emphasize a different type of question each time. For instance, I may have more True/False on one exam, then more Multiple Choice on another, or more Short Answer/Essay. I want to play to the myriad of learning styles for each student. It is certainly not an ideal solution for reaching all types of learning styles but in a small way maybe the student will comprehend more and do better on exams by my emphasizing question variety.

One concept that Quintilian put forth was the idea that "it is the duty of the master to teach, so it is the duty of the pupil to show himself teachable." I remind students of that all of the time by asking them how prepared they are for class, if they read the material, if they did the assignment, and if they are prepared to learn. They realize that we are all in this together and I promise to be prepared, but they must commit to being prepared also.

Whether they are new faculty, post-docs, adjunct or part-time instructors, postgraduate students or from the professional fields, new teachers are seeking to understand and negotiate their new roles and identities. While they will bring a wide range of background, skills and experience to their new positions, they may know very little about what teaching in higher education entails beyond knowledge of their own content area. Their prior opportunities to engage in teaching may have been very limited. As postgraduate or graduate students, they may have served as teaching assistants, supporting a faculty member. Those in professional schools, such as journalists, doctors, engineers, and artists, will have been immersed in what they do, but may not have done much teaching except in a very ad hoc way. Of course, novice teachers are beset by the same pressures that plague other teachers in higher education: poor teacher-student ratios, declining resources and competing demands of research, teaching, service, and administration (Light, Cox, & Calkins, 2009).

Attitude is Everything!

Finally, in one study, teachers frequently mentioned the need to maintain a positive outlook. When giving advice to new teachers on how to preserve their enthusiasm for teaching, one teacher shared the following: "Talk to other teachers, especially teachers who are positive, not ones that are negative. And everybody's negative some days, but there's always somebody that's happy about being a teacher, and you have to find that one." Also, putting the students first seemed to create a source of intrinsic satisfaction. When teachers realize the powerful impact they have on their students and the world in general, their sense of passion remains. With this perspective, it becomes easier to maintain a positive attitude.

Another characteristic of teachers who maintain their passion for the education profession are those who seek and embrace change. Teachers who last more than a few years are open to change, engage in professional development, have a learner perspective, reach out to colleagues for support, and engage in self-reflection/examination (Phelps & Benson, 2012).

Summary

In summary, if you get the "calling" to teach whether sooner or later in life, please explore it. There are students who need dedicated, caring, enthusiastic teachers to guide them along life's path. You may want to take the survey at the end of this book to help determine if you have a propensity for teaching.

CHAPTER 7

FACULTY

Faculty members come to the community college through a variety of routes, most often not as an intended career option (Fugate & Amey, 2000). Indeed, Townsend and Twombly (2007) underscore the varied pathways to faculty ranks at two-year colleges and point out that possession of a Ph.D. is gaining traction, but that the master's degree remains the most popular, desired degree in the sector.

The master's degree is required of those who teach transfer-level courses. As just mentioned, it is the most common educational credential of full-time community college faculty members. In 2003, 63 percent of full-time community college faculty members teaching one or more credit courses held the master's as their highest degree, while more than 19 percent held the doctorate, 1.9 percent a professional degree, almost 12 percent the bachelor's degree, and 3.9 percent an associate's degree or equivalent (Rosser & Townsend, 2006).

Can just anyone teach? Possibly, but it is important to realize that there is a difference between the skills required for classroom teaching and being a content expert. New faculty needs support in figuring out their roles: how to work with diverse learners, use active learning and cooperative learning to help in classroom teaching, evaluate student learning, and be a good colleague (Eddy, 2010). We all have had experiences where an expert who is very good at their job cannot translate that expertise into teaching the skill. Teaching is acquired from research, knowledge, observation, experience, and a basic caring for students who are attempting to better their lives.

Employed Full- or Part-time
Community colleges are generally more inclusive to female faculty as compared to four-year institutions. Women represent 49 percent of full-time and 50 percent of part-time community college faculty, a stark contrast to the low numbers of female faculty in four-year institutions (Cataldi, Fahimi, & Bradburn, 2005).

There is a substantial divide in higher education among the working conditions found in various segments (Levinson, 2003). Faculty at community colleges are more likely than those in other sectors of higher education to be nontenured and to work in an institution that does not have a tenure system; to be part-time; to have a larger teaching load (fifteen credit hours is the norm for full-time faculty); and not to possess a terminal degree in their discipline. Community college faculty constitute a more temporary workforce than their counterparts at baccalaureate institutions (Parsad & Glover, 2002).

In keeping with the mission, community college faculty members' primary responsibility is teaching. In addition, faculty members reserve an average 9.2 hours per week for office hours and serve as academic advisers to students, helping them plan their programs of study. Faculty members also work with students as sponsors of clubs, community service projects, newspapers, literary publications, and other extracurricular activities.

Part-time faculty play an important role in assisting the community college to be a comprehensive institution of higher education by bringing specialties to the college that may not be available among full-time faculty. For example, most colleges would not have a full-time faculty member available to teach courses in real estate, whereas qualified instructors are readily available in any community with a viable real estate market. Similarly, a local banker can bring practical experience to the community college classroom that might be unavailable among full-time faculty (Vaughan, 2000).

Technical vs. Academic Teaching

I like the technical aspect of a community college education because I am a pragmatist and if I cannot see the logic and application then I lose interest quickly. My normal teaching load is 5 classes, or 15 hours. I have almost always taught more than 5 classes because it helps me stay refreshed, it helps the students who need to take the class and it involves extra pay. A teaching load is a balancing act because you need to know when you have overextended yourself. There certainly comes a point where a teacher is not effective when teaching too many classes. At that point, I have to question his/her motives. We can all sign up for teaching countless classes but when class preparation falls by the wayside and you are only driven by making extra money then it is time to cut back your teaching load. I've seen it happen many times and the student is the one who pays the price. Of course, a lot depends on the number of preparations you have. For instance, I usually teach 6-7 classes which includes 4 or 5 preparations (I've found that 5 preps is my limit). Whereas, teaching academic courses you may have only one preparation. For instance, a Speech teacher may teach 5 sections of Speech and only have one preparation. The advantage to that is knowing your material extremely well and not having to prepare as much because you can focus on one subject. The disadvantage is staying motivated. I could not imagine anything more mundane than teaching five sections of the same course. I would probably go crazy! That is why I am thankful to be on the technical side of community college teaching because it keeps me refreshed. I initially started teaching Business classes only; courses such as: Human Relations, Introduction to Business, Principles of Marketing, and Principles of Management. After two years with the college, I went back to graduate school and earned 18 hours in Communication Studies which added Speech to my repertoire. It was a great challenge and it kept me fresh and motivated for my Business classes. I thoroughly enjoyed teaching Speech for 20 years, but I have since moved on to teaching Developmental Math. The Math seems to afford more application than did Speech. I see immediate results when we are solving problems or learning a new technique. "Light bulb" moments excite me!

My job description is to teach Business courses and I have accepted that, but it certainly helps to have a variety of courses to teach. Teaching outside your department is also a great recruiting tool! Many students in Speech wound up taking Business classes with me. Then too, it recruits students for other colleague's classes. Since they are already on campus for Speech, for instance, they are more likely to stay and enroll in other classes as well. It will also make you more valuable to your college because you can fill in if they need a teacher for some other area that you are qualified to teach in. It is good job security and I thrive on variety. For example, I admire English teachers so much for their tenacity and determination. They have to grade essay after essay and it takes a lot

of determination and commitment to help students and also stay
motivated themselves.

Playing Your Role

Are you a team player? I do not think it is critical to be a
team player because it is generally you and the students in the
classroom, though it does help to be a team player outside the
classroom. You will be working with scheduling and in deciding
who will teach which course at what times. You will need to run
trial schedules to coordinate course offerings. For example, a
student usually would not take Business Law and Human Relations
the same semester so you might offer those courses in the same time
slot, and so on. Will you teach some night classes? Do you prefer
morning classes? Also, a colleague may call in sick and you may
have to cover their class? There will be meetings and you might be
on a committee with some colleagues. So it helps to be a team
player and as in any business, it is certainly much more pleasant
working when you get along well with co-workers. We have an
annual fund called "Esprit de Corps," where the faculty is asked to
donate a minimum of $10 each fall semester to help pay for cards,
flowers, and other things needed when someone is sick or dies
throughout the school year. There are several people who never
contribute. Why, is beyond me. Shouldn't you support the place in
which you work? There will be children of faculty members selling
all sorts of things for fundraisers and I believe we owe it to them to
buy something. It is part of being a team player. Sure, there are
things I have bought through the years that I really didn't need but I
either donated them to charity or gave them to someone who could
use them. In that sense, you need to be a team player. In another
instance, we just had a colleague retire and we collected money for
her gift. Unfortunately, about 40% of faculty and staff did not
contribute. I truly do not understand that.

The Beach Boys tune "Be True to Your School," should be a
college anthem. I was shocked to learn that our scholarship fund
only has about a 20% participation rate by faculty and staff. The
scholarship fund can be contributed to by payroll deductions and
when I get a raise I increase my contribution a bit so I will never
miss money I do not yet have. This is another part of being a team
player. Be true to your school and if you want to call it playing

games, then so be it. I am most grateful to have a job and career that I love and I am happy and proud to give back. Monetary participation results in helping more students attend college and some of those will be in your classes, so it is a win-win proposition. Just do it!

With an average work week of not quite fifty hours, including paid and unpaid institutional tasks and tasks outside the community college, the typical full-time instructor spends about 85 percent of his or her time on instruction, including advising students, grading papers, and preparing for classes. In contrast, full-time faculty members at comprehensive colleges and universities report spending about 73 percent of their time on instruction, while university faculty members report spending almost 66 percent (Rosser & Townsend, 2006).

Community colleges commonly have written and published standards or criteria to guide decisions regarding faculty appointments, contract renewals, promotions, and the granting and termination of tenure. Since they often constitute the contract between the faculty member and the college (thus binding the college), such evaluative standards and criteria should receive the careful attention of administrators and faculty members alike (Rodriguez, 2010).

Promotion to a higher rank depends at a minimum on time in previous rank, educational credentials, and teaching performance. In some states faculty members teaching transfer-level courses typically need a doctorate to advance to full professor, while faculty teaching occupational-technical courses typically need a master's degree. The ease or difficulty in achieving a promotion in rank is not clear, as almost nothing has been written about this topic (Kelly, 1990).

Regarding job titles, you will probably start with the title of Instructor, then depending on length of service and educational achievements you will promote to Assistant Professor, then Associate Professor, and finally Professor. At South Plains College, to be a Professor requires either a doctorate or 20 or more years in the profession (depending on the vote of the Rank/Promotion committee). Unfortunately, our rank promotions do not include a raise in pay. But, hey, it's a title! Receiving tenure takes 4-7 years. The instructor is reviewed thoroughly and a committee votes whether to grant tenure. I have never seen tenure as a particular advantage but some colleagues think it is huge. Tenure basically says you can only be terminated for just cause or if they terminate your program altogether. It is a form of job security.

Tenure

Tenure is mutually beneficial for the faculty member and for the institution. Tenure gives the faculty member job security and the institution a sense of employee stability. As defined by the American Association of University Professors in 1940, tenure served as the way to ensure academic freedom "through an employment contract that guaranteed permanent or continuous employment and due process in the event of termination for cause" (Gappa et al., 2007). Yes, tenured professors can still be released, but the institution must follow due process and have a cause for release. Before tenure is granted, institutions may release instructors and professors without stating cause--a contract is simply not renewed (Clement, 2010). So, before receiving tenure, the instructor is basically in a probationary period the same way a business can release an employee within the first 30-90 days of employment without any repercussions.

Professional Development

What about professional development? How do we keep ourselves "fresh" regarding material and teaching methods? The proudest claim of community colleges has always been that they are student-centered teaching institutions. As community colleges were largely shaped by this vision, so also their faculties developed professional identities divorced from scholarship and disciplines, new identities as effective teachers, the vanguard of an instructional revolution. With this came a new notion of faculty development; the new profession was to be single-mindedly concerned with the improvement of instruction. In keeping with that orientation, the most common professional development activities at community colleges purport to help individual faculty members improve their teaching (McGrath & Spear, 1994).

Though some faculty manage to maintain a productive schedule of scholarly work outside of teaching, others find that the time constraints posed by heavy teaching loads take their toll. In unsolicited comments, many respondents emphasized the imposing burdens born by teachers who face 150 or more students per semester, many of whom have deficiencies in the basic skills. Some commented that the work-a-day grind is intellectually debilitating. For example, a philosophy instructor with several years' experience wrote that "the problem with the community college is we teach too much--repeat ourselves too often and don't have enough time and energy to refuel." Another respondent noted that after years of teaching five courses per term, including summers, he had "gotten out of the habit of being scholarly." For many faculty members, though not all, time constraints posed by heavy teaching loads stifled intellectual life, making it more difficult for faculty to remain active scholars as they progress through their careers (Palmer, 1994).

There are many reasons to consider professional development as an important part of career development. Professional development falls into two categories, that of personal development and institutionally led development. It is important to appreciate that the two are inextricably linked, and that overall individual and institutional development cannot occur in isolation from each other. This has been written about as the learning organization, one which takes the view that "if institutions are about promoting the learning of students in a changing world and learning is worthwhile and not about a static or bounded process, then the learning of educational professionals throughout their career is essential" (Craft, 1996). This suggests that as teachers we have to continually learn in order to cope with the increasing demands for change within higher education. Would you want to take your car to a mechanic whose skills are outdated? Of course not! Then, we, as teachers, must constantly take advantage of learning/training opportunities to upgrade our knowledge, our approach, our teaching style, and teach students to the best of our abilities. I mentioned earlier that it is easy to fall into the same old routine and same lecture notes you've used for years. Colleges usually will have professional development accessible to faculty, but we must also make the effort to upgrade on our own.

Summary

In summary, the teaching profession is not for everyone. We discussed "the calling" to teach in the last chapter and that is great if you feel that. We reviewed the ins and outs of being a faculty member regarding the community college mission, average workload, job descriptions, being a team player, and the need for professional development. All of this contributes to being the best teacher/professor possible and being a good role model in the community to help recruit students and promote the community college as a great avenue to higher education.

CHAPTER 8

ETHICS/PROFESSIONALISM

Throughout this book you may have gotten the impression that not a lot of policing takes place regarding faculty. I agree with that impression. What I am saying is that, as faculty, there is trust inherent in the position. As mentioned earlier, you can pretty much come and go as you please as long as you teach your classes. Let your conscience be your guide. I know better than anyone if I am not putting much effort into my teaching, or if I am not dressed to properly represent my profession.

Ethics is defined as a moral standard of right and wrong. Although the definition of ethics is a simple statement, it is important to identify who and what determines what is morally right and wrong. Ethical behavior is a reflection of the influences of friends, family, coworkers, religion, and society (Anderson & Bolt, 2013).

Each person's personal code of ethics is determined by a combination of factors. We start to form ethical standards as children in response to our perceptions of the behavior of parents and other adults. Soon, we enter school, where we're influenced by peers, and as we grow into adulthood, experience shapes our lives and contributes to our ethical beliefs and our behavior. We also develop values and morals that contribute to ethical standards. If you put financial gain at the top of your priority list, you may develop a code of ethics that supports the pursuit of material comfort. If you set family and friends as a priority, you'll no doubt adopt different standards (Ebert & Griffin, 2013). Certainly get your priorities straight before you attempt teaching. Do you like taking shortcuts? Doing as little as possible to get by? Do you believe in giving a full day's work for a full day's pay? There will be many situations in your teaching career where your ethics/morals will be put on display so set your course on the straight and narrow and you'll never be disappointed.

In the role of teacher, people are expected to teach and fairly evaluate student learning. Thus, misrepresentation by teachers can include inattentive planning and a cynical attitude toward teaching, while misbehavior by teachers may include unarticulated or ambiguous expectations and personal disregard (for example, consistently being late to class). These misbehaviors can manifest themselves by acting in ways that are not overtly misconduct but are counter to prevailing behavioral expectations (Gallant, 2008).

Remember when you took a college class and you really had no choice but to trust that the professor would be fair. If a classmate was absent, continually tardy, or disruptive, then it was expected that that student would be penalized in some way. Well, I am required to take attendance and since part of the overall course grade is attached to that, then a few absences do cost the student some overall points. It's imperative that students trust us and that we not betray that trust. It is true that the student should only be concerned with his/her own grade, but inevitably they notice and compare. Believe me, word spreads quickly if you are not fair in your grading, or you play favorites.

Drawing Boundaries

What about socializing with students? Interactions between instructors and their students will not be restricted to the classroom, nor should they be. Discussing course material during office hours and providing guidance regarding academic matters are important ways in which instructors contribute to the student's education. Difficulties can arise when teacher-student relationships are mixed with social interactions. Students like teachers who are friendly and easy to talk to, who appear interested in students. For instructors, breaking through the anonymity of class rosters and having pleasant conversations with students makes teaching much more enjoyable and fulfilling. Having good rapport with students increases the effectiveness of class meetings--students pay more attention to what is being said, and students' participation increases. There is no sensible criticism of students and teachers liking one another. Questions concern the kinds of social behavior that are acceptable. Please note, the key here is POWER! Because instructors are in the power position and students are not, responsibility for keeping relationships within acceptable limits falls undoubtedly on the shoulder of instructors. Teachers want to be liked--perhaps new teachers especially want students to like them as a sign that their teaching is going well. However, instructors must keep in mind that they are not teaching classes to be liked, that their primary mission is to teach. Unlike ordinary friendships, which are between equals, student-teacher relationships are unbalanced; instructors need to keep this in mind (Dominowski, 2002).

Wow! The previous paragraph discusses two important concepts. First, all teachers want to be liked, but we must develop a thick skin and realize that we are there first and foremost to TEACH! There will be some students who like you and others who don't, it comes with the job. The second, and more important concept, is that of power. The teacher has the power, the student does not. If I ask a student to meet me for socializing after classroom hours, then it opens up all sorts of negative possibilities. The student is afraid to say no because it might affect their course grade (they have no power). Also, if the student agrees to meet after hours, then what if other students see you together? What if the relationship sours and the student complains to your department chair or dean? Is this whole scenario worth possibly having administration investigate you, or worse yet, losing your job? Be friendly and approachable to your students but be ethical and professional in your teaching responsibilities.

A Matter of Autonomy and Trust

I mentioned earlier working as an insurance adjuster, and for many years management would fly into town unbeknownst to me, and wait at the post office the next morning to see when I started my day. They would also follow behind me to check shops that I had just left. It seemed odd to me that they trusted me with thousands of dollars and a company car, yet they didn't trust me to do my job properly. I had a wide open operation and they could find whatever they wanted that needed correcting.

After being trained in such a manner (Theory X style management) I was pleasantly surprised when I started working at South Plains College. There was no one checking to see if I was keeping my office hours or preparing for class. It was nice to be trusted, finally (Theory Y style management). It took a semester or two before I relaxed a bit and probably became a better teacher. Don't you find so often that if you live up to your personal standards that they far exceed company standards? I know if I'm doing the best I can then there should be no productivity worries on my part. It's a good feeling, indeed!

Last semester I noticed a teacher continually arrive at least 10-15 minutes after the class was scheduled to begin. I don't know if she could not be here on time for some reason or if she told students that's when class would begin? Not only is it against school policy, but it also sets a bad precedent. I taught an 8 a.m. class where some students continually arrived late. I was perplexed as to why anyone would sign up for a class they knew they couldn't get to on time. I first lectured them about not signing up for an early class if they could not arrive on schedule—that didn't work. Then, I threatened to count two tardies as an absence—that didn't work. After scratching my brain, I decided to give the answer to one of the test questions after taking roll at the beginning of class as a reward for being punctual. I told students they could give the answer to the late-comers if they chose to, but it was up to them. I was totally surprised how tight-lipped they were and even more surprised that by the third exam everyone was arriving on time for class.

It is all about being professional and doing your job. Some faculty members take vacations during the semester, thus missing class time, and I have no clue as to why. Other faculty must cover their classes and it can become a burden. We should be committed to teaching and being there for students the entire semester. With summers off, holidays, and weeks between semesters, is there any excuse for faculty missing class (other than illness)?

Do I need a doctorate to teach here? No. My job requirements are a Master's degree including graduate hours in Business with work experience also. Remember, like any job, that if you do something above and beyond job requirements to better yourself that's great. But do not expect your employer to make special allowances for you.

Little institutional support exists for community college faculty members wishing to do research defined in the traditional way as disciplinary scholarship resulting in new knowledge and publication. The institution rarely provides release time to do research, although some provide sabbatical leaves for completing doctoral work. Most colleges also support faculty travel to conferences to deliver papers (Murray, 2001).

I remember staying up until the wee hours of the morning typing my dissertation and I had to be at school by 8 a.m. the next day. When you meet the minimum requirements (usually a Master's degree) and you are hired, then anything beyond that is up to you. Do not expect favors or time off because you are working on a doctorate. The Dean and I had made about the same progress in graduate school and I called her one morning at school about a question I had. I then found out that she had taken the day off to work on her dissertation. It was a bit unfair, because as a faculty member I did not have that luxury. Students are waiting in class for you and you must be prepared, regardless of what you do outside of school.

As a side note here, make sure to pass along compliments you hear. We all like positive reinforcement and when I hear a positive comment about an instructor I tell them. I hear student comments in the hallway and I always try to pass them on to the instructor. Who the student is does not matter; it is the compliment that matters. It helps us know that we are doing something right and that is always a good feeling. Certainly do not pass along negative comments. It will only put you in a bad light with colleagues and if you are suddenly not included in the lunch group on Fridays you will know why.

Professionalism

Professionalism is defined as workplace behaviors that result in positive business relationships (Anderson & Bolt, 2013). To me, professionalism is a bit different from ethics because professionalism is more outward conduct, and ethics deals with inner beliefs and values, but they are closely related. Professionalism is acting the part of a professional, whether in business or teaching. It is conducting yourself in a manner that reflects positively on you and your institution. Rising above the fray and looking at the overall good is the epitome of professionalism. Yelling at a student in class, not being prepared, showing up late for class, and not meeting college deadlines are all examples of not being professional. I had a colleague (no longer employed by the college) who started cussing at students in class and occasionally didn't even show up for class. He was called in, talked to, and given another chance but ending up resigning his position. I don't know if he cracked or just didn't care anymore. Again, this is not a job for the meek because you will be tested every way possible.

College teachers spend so much time teaching solo behind the closed doors of their classroom that this isolation can induce in them a distorted perception of their own failings. When teachers talk together in staff meetings, their conversations usually concern administrative necessities and procedures. Rarely do they talk about the rhythms and dilemmas of their day-to-day teaching practices. Yet, private and informal talks with your peers about situations that confound you usually reveal that these situations are equally confounding to others! Realizing that other colleagues regard themselves as inept and inadequate—the same way you regard yourself—is enormously reassuring (Brookfield, 2006). Getting to know your colleagues is very important for that reason. Simply visiting with colleagues in their office can open up new visions of what we are doing in the classroom and if it is successful.

Summary
In summary, ethics and professionalism boils down to commitment, effort, role modeling, and caring. If you can look in the mirror with a clear conscience at day's end, then you can be proud of the job you've done. What is your work ethic? Do you believe in an honest day's work for an honest day's pay? Or, do you believe in exerting the least amount of effort possible? Do you believe that faculty should be solid role models for students? Do you live up to your own high standards? These are some of the questions that need answers before exploring a teaching career.

CHAPTER 9

STUDENTS

The growing diversity of the student body is another challenge that is expected to continue over the next 20 to 30 years, based on population projections. One group of students includes recent high school graduates who plan to transfer to baccalaureate-granting institutions. Another group is somewhat older, often lacks basic skills and English language skills, and seeks job skills for immediate entry into the workforce. Yet another group is composed of workers who want to diversify or upgrade job skills through either credit or noncredit study. Finally, there is a group that seeks enrichment through coursework and recreational or cultural activities. Of course, these groups include both men and women and people of all colors, abilities, academic preparation, and ages. Community colleges must address the lifelong learning demands of all these groups through a comprehensive array of services that is constantly being adjusted.

As under-represented populations increasingly enroll in community colleges it is important to note that they may be the first ones in their family to pursue a college degree. These students have no guides or coaches at home, no one to help them navigate a system that is often set up for the convenience of the faculty and staff rather than the convenience of the students. Many of these students have complex personal and educational needs that the institution is unable to identify much less meet, and they do not learn the way earlier students have learned, i.e., by listening to lectures and taking notes. To add to the challenge, a small percentage are underprepared and unmotivated, even though they have earned high school equivalency status (Culp, 1998).

Staying Current

The contemporary community college is also challenged by the need to maintain the currency of curricula in light of workforce preparation mandates, competition from other education providers, and the globalized economy. New programs appear almost daily as colleges develop programs that prepare workers for emerging career fields, such as information technology security and homeland security (Phillippe & Sullivan, 2005, p. 5). My college recently initiated a program in wind energy support services and also digital forensics in the computer information systems area. Also, this last semester I worked with the Automotive Technology coordinator in implementing a certificate program for service writers in auto dealerships. The trend is to train service writers in business and human relations skills because they deal directly with customers and retaining those customers is crucial, especially nowadays.

Different Needs

In a study at Bakersfield College in Kern County, California the students interviewed described traditional aged students (18 to 24, i.e., young people who graduated from high school and were living alone or with their parents) as individuals who lacked educational goals and a perspective of their future occupational life. When young students enrolled in a college program, they tended to be uncertain about what they wanted to pursue as an educational pathway to a career. Most of the traditional aged students saw transferring to a university as their main educational goal; however, they were unclear about the reasons underlying such a goal or how they could accomplish it. Students knew that they wanted to transfer to a four-year institution; however they were unaware of the major that they wanted to pursue and the reasons for that choice. These traditionally aged students also exhibited educational deficiencies and lack of knowledge about how to deal with the academic and administrative affairs concerning their identity as community college students (Levin & Montero-Hernandez, 2009). Isn't this further evidence that we must be good counselors and advisors to help students reach their potential?

Hamm (2004) observes that in contrast with traditional students at four-year colleges and universities, most community college students are torn by multiple roles. The majority work full-time. Almost 30 percent of community college students are married, and over one-third have at least one dependent (Wilson, 2004) and 7 percent are single parents. In addition, many are new to higher education (39 percent are the first generation to attend college). Almost four in ten community college students have parents who did not attend any postsecondary institution. These students tend to have lower educational expectations. Completion of a certificate is more likely to be a primary educational goal than transferring to senior institutions (Wilson, 2004).

When I started teaching at the community college, it was an eye-opening experience. There are students who have serious problems that I was certainly not aware of. When I was a university student living in the dorm I had no reason to miss class unless I was really ill. But here, we have single parents who are sick or their kids are sick. They are working two jobs or more and they cannot buy their books until they get the next paycheck. The community college is definitely a different setting and atmosphere than a university. I see more need here and students struggling to deal with everyday life than I would ever have imagined. I teach at a branch campus so our demographics are a bit different than the main campus.

Challenging Them

At my campus our student body averages 27-28 years old vs. 20-21 years old on the main campus. Many of our students are working full or part-time. I also teach night classes and they are filled with mostly non-traditional students (age 25 and over) who are working full-time. I like teaching both morning and evening because the morning classes are younger students who need a bit more nurturing and discipline. My night class students are more focused because they are working and going to school to better their lives. Most night school students do not have to be told twice and are usually on time with assignments. I do like the balance between day and night classes because it challenges and stretches my teaching style.

In talking about students between the main campus and our branch campus, it is interesting to note some differences between generations also. Okay, here goes "when I was a student" discussion! When I was a student I seldom blamed the teacher for my poor grade. Nowadays, students complain that the test was tricky or that my review was not complete enough. Also, in my days as a student, if I had not prepared for class, I tried to fake it or hope the teacher wouldn't call my name. Nowadays, my students are so honest that they usually tell me at the beginning of class that they hadn't read the chapter. Their honesty is refreshing, but amusing. If it were me, I'd still try to fake it.

Allow me to further reminisce as I remember back to sixth grade in Mrs. Burnside's English class. I told my older brother, whom I looked up to, that I had to do a book report. He advised me not to waste time reading the book, but to simply read the first and last pages and make up the story in between. He reasoned that the teacher had so many papers to grade that chances were she had never read the book. Did I mention that my older brother's advice occasionally got me into trouble? Well, I chose Thor Heyerdahl's "Kon-Tiki," and I thought I'd made up a pretty decent story. I was rather proud of myself, until Mrs. Burnside passed the book reports back. Mine had an "F" on it and she asked me to stay after class. I'll never forget her calm demeanor as I stood before her desk and she asked, "Mr. Wilhelm, did you read that book?" I knew I was toast at that point and there was no use in digging the hole deeper. I answered, "No, ma'am." She then gave me the choice of keeping the "F" or doing another book report for a "D." I did another book report! I learned an unforgettable lesson that day from an understanding, compassionate teacher and I seldom took my big brother's advice again.

The lesson here is that as a teacher, you will have students who will invent ways to get out of work. How will you handle them? Will you give them another chance? I have never understood students who attempt to cheat on exams. They spend so much time coming up with creative ways to cheat that it would have been less time consuming to just study the material.

When I taught Speech, we worked on resume writing and I was invariably asked about listing any type of prison record in the student's background. I've always thought that it was a matter of opinion, but that they had better be prepared to explain that time gap if they chose not to list it. Of course, they will have to put it on the job application where it asks about felonies or a criminal record. The old saying, "honesty is the best policy," certainly rings true in this case. If the student omits their criminal record on the job application, then they are lying, and will be fired after the background check is completed. How does this relate to you as a teacher? Well, the point I am making is most students will be honest, but we also owe it to them to disseminate useful, accurate information. I will reiterate that the community college student is a totally different being than you would encounter in a high school or university setting, with totally different needs and motivations. I know that one of my biggest teaching challenges is being flexible and patient.

Being a commuter college, we sometimes have bad weather days and classes are cancelled because of road conditions. It is something that cannot be planned for but it would be wise to build some flexibility into your schedule. I usually add a workday each semester to the syllabus and then I can either use that day to catch up, if we had a weather cancellation, or use the day for discussion or a video.

Entering college entails exposure to specific academic and social environments where faculty and students hold particular beliefs and expectations of themselves and others. Having faculty members who are perceived by students as being approachable and having high standards and expectations is associated with greater learning. Students' perceptions of these faculty attributes are related: faculty members who have high expectations also tend to have high standards and are approachable. If we consider all three of these faculty attributes simultaneously, high expectations stand out as the only relevant factor, and are thus a particularly salient aspect of educational experience which is associated with students' learning. A prominent sociological tradition of status attainment over the past forty years has highlighted how expectations of significant others, including teachers, are important for facilitating students' educational success. This still holds true on college campuses today: when faculty have high expectations, students learn more (Sewell, Haller, & Portes, 1969).

What About Expectations?

An expectation is a huge concept in any relationship and it certainly applies in the classroom. What do we expect of students? What do they expect of us? Contrary to some student beliefs, the classroom is not a democracy. We announce our expectations of students in the syllabus. The syllabus defines the course and is the guide that we must live by. It spells out how the course grade will be determined from exams, projects, participation, and so on. The only choice a student has is to choose to drop the course and sign up with a different teacher next semester if he/she feels they cannot abide by the rules in the syllabus. What about student expectations of teachers?

Shouldn't we be asking students what they expect of us? I ask my students what they expect of not only me but of teachers in general. I write their expectations on the board and it is great discussion material to start students participating. Many of them relate stories of classroom experiences and I keep the board list as my guide throughout the semester. I get variations of the following list:

1. Be accessible.
2. Know the subject matter.
3. Show up, be punctual.
4. Be prepared.
5. Understand student problems.
6. Teach at a level conducive to learning.
7. Keep office hours.
8. Have a sense of humor.
9. Be patient.
10. Give timely feedback.
11. Be respectful.
12. Lead by example.
13. Be on a first name basis.

In communicating with students in the classroom, instructors need to monitor their behavior so that they communicate with students in all parts of the room. Some students will be more active, ask better questions, and give more frequent or better answers to questions posed to the class. Because these student behaviors are reinforcing to instructors, there's a tendency for instructors to direct much of their presentation to especially active students. What is required is that instructors give other students ample opportunity to participate in the class. Patience is required, as well as encouragement of students who might be reluctant to speak out in public situations. It is also important to be gentle in responding to students' comments, questions, and answers. Students are reluctant to speak in classes because they fear looking foolish or uninformed. The worst thing that can happen is for the instructor to react negatively to a student's statement, that is, to give the impression that he or she considers the student to be foolish or uninformed.

Instructors need to walk a delicate line, balancing gentle encouragement of students' participation with accurate and clarifying responses to the content of what students say. No good will come from students' forming the impressions that the instructor treats some students better than others (Dominowski, 2002).

Get to know your colleagues as soon as possible and choose one as your mentor. I was lucky to have, as my mentor, the other Business teacher. He would answer all of my questions and keep me out of trouble. Unfortunately, he retired a few years ago but I still recall him telling me to get in the habit of never closing my office door when a female student entered. He told me of an instance where one of his female students started gossip that she was dating him. Needless to say, the college investigated and found nothing. The female student ended up admitting that she made the story up to make her boyfriend jealous. Wow! I initially thought that it was kind of silly advice and that it would never happen to me but to this day, I heed his advice whenever a female student enters my office.

Community college faculty members teach many students who take credit courses for a variety of reasons other than preparation for transfer to a four-year school. According to a study by VanDerLinden (2002), only 21 percent of students attend community college with transfer as their only goal, although another 24 percent attend partly for future transfer but also for developing their mind and enriching their life. Career concerns are the motivation for most other students. Almost 30 percent attend to prepare for a career, while 11 percent seek to upgrade their skills so they can advance in their careers. Additionally, some students attend to take noncredit courses in developmental education or noncredit continuing education courses for their personal enrichment or career upgrading.

Cheating

What about cheating in the classroom? The following is a bit different slant on the subject but it certainly is an interesting viewpoint. Some authors have suggested that academic misconduct may be less about the failures of students and more about the failures of instructors and institutions to rethink teaching and learning in this "new electronic environment" (Townley & Parsell, 2004). This failure to rethink teaching and learning could in part be an outcome of the excessive concern with protecting the grading and evaluation systems from student corruption.

Take, for example, the use of a cell phone to obtain answers while taking an exam. Most would consider this practice a blatant act of academic misconduct in a system that depends on the use of examinations to test a student's independent knowledge and abilities. And in such an educational system, the act should be considered misconduct and treated accordingly because it is not fair to those students who completed the exam independently without cheating. At the same time, this practice raises some interesting considerations beyond stopping the student from cheating. For instance, how is technology, with its capabilities to connect people and resources, slowly changing what and how students should be learning? Will students need to attend college or university in the future to receive knowledge from experts or be tested on the ability to apply what one has memorized? How is technology changing the forms of evaluations that should be used? These questions are just some of the intriguing ones that emerge when considering academic integrity as a teaching and learning imperative. Thus, as campuses continue to work to enhance academic integrity, it may be time to also reconsider methods for teaching and assessment that work with rather than fight against the digital world of the future (Gallant, 2008).

Summary

In summary, community colleges are open access for a reason. You will be faced with far different challenges than if you were teaching at the high school or university level, but students need us. They need us as reservoirs of knowledge and application and also as role models, coaches, and guides. Having high expectations for your students is essential in any teaching arena and most students will attain the goals we set for them.

CHAPTER 10

TECHNOLOGY/ONLINE COURSES

The first reason for online college classes is that there are simply too many students entering higher education to be accommodated by traditional offerings. As record numbers of students start college, there are not enough seats available.

The next reason is that students, and their expectations, have changed. We all know some students who do not want to attend 8 a.m. classes or classes at other times that they deem inconvenient. This is the "I want it my way" generation. So, they sleep late, hit a few classes, work at the 30-hour-a-week job, and then attend class online at a time when it is convenient—between midnight and 3 a.m. The idea that a discussion can be online, like texting their friends, appeals to some students. While this example is a bit stereotypic, today's students do want a lot of flexibility, and watching the professor's lecture from their apartment at 2 a.m. appeals to many students (Clement, 2010).

Certainly, college students today – millennials specifically – are extremely comfortable with technology, and generally view its existence as part of their natural living environment. Computers, the Internet, email and social networking systems (e.g., 'Facebook', 'Twitter') are considered an expected part of everyday life; as such, students may be quicker to experience or see the potential application of new technologies than their teachers (Oblinger, 2003). Students' ease with technology, and seeming impatience with older or outdated technologies, may intimidate faculty unnecessarily. Pressured faculty may either seize on technological 'bells and whistles' in the hopes of catching their students' attention, or ignore technology altogether, clinging to traditional assumptions about learning (Light, Cox, & Calkins, 2009).

Online learning allows students to study from the comfort of their home or office. As reported by the Sloan Consortium (Bourne & Moore, 2003), the most effective online learning is that which students perceive as personalized and engaging. In 2003, 90 percent of public community colleges offered online learning, the highest percentage of any higher education segment in the United States (Waits & Lewis, 2003).

Besides offering courses that are fully online, community colleges are also engaged in enhancing existing courses through technology, whether it be through hybrid courses (courses offered via an array of instructional modalities, most often as a combination of in-class didactic and distance learning, typically alternating class sessions between the two) or Web-enhanced courses (in which an instructor makes heavy use of a companion Web site where students engage in online chats, access supplemental course materials, and in general extend the classroom beyond the traditional brick-and-mortar context) (Levinson, 2005, pp. 103-4).

Classroom vs. Digital Deliverance

The major differences between online and campus courses can be summarized in five characteristics:

1. *The faculty role shifts to coaching and mentoring.* A faculty's role in online courses is primarily coaching, mentoring, guiding, and directing learning rather than lecturing and telling. Online courses are more of a bottom-up development of knowledge that require learners to interact with one another and the content resources to construct their knowledge rather than relying on the trickle-down delivery of content from an instructor. This is actually good, as more research is indicating that lecturing is an inefficient way of learning. In most lectures, learners are too passive for much higher-level learning to occur (McKeachie, Pintrich, Lin, & Smith, 1986; Wieman, 2008). This shift means that you as an instructor do not have to spend a great deal of time preparing for live lectures. The time for teaching a course shifts to preparing short mini-lectures and introductions, preparing facilitation and community building experiences, and monitoring and guiding students in their learning experiences.

2. *Meetings are asynchronous.* Online class discussions are primarily asynchronous—at different times—rather than synchronous—at the same time. Since online discussions are asynchronous and require learners' comments and statements, there is an

unwritten requirement that learners reflect on what they have learned from the resource assignments before they come to class (online) to participate in the course activities, such as posting their responses in the discussion areas. The online classrooms now provide opportunities for synchronous gatherings, but good online practice uses this for discussions, question-and-answer sessions, collaborative project work, and presentations.

3. *Learners are more active.* Learners' dialogue and activity are increased in online courses. Learners must do more thinking, writing, doing, sharing, reflecting, and peer reviewing as part of a community of learners. Students often come to a campus class without completing the reading assignment and expect that the instructor will enlighten them, saving themselves time. Learners in an online course cannot hide passively. If they have not prepared and processed the content prior to posting their discussion responses, that shortcoming is evident to everyone. Learners are therefore motivated to complete the reading to interact well with the others. This change means that faculty must design discussion forums with effective catalyst discussion questions before the course begins.

4. *Learning resources and spaces are more flexible.* Content resources are now increasingly mobile, accessible on smartphones, iPods, and other small, mobile, hand-held devices. This means that learners have many more options than in the past as to when, where, and with whom they work on course goals. Too much flexibility can encourage lax participation, so establishing a weekly rhythm and regular milestones is essential. The world of content resources is also much expanded. In addition to the usual mix of required, highly recommended, and other resources, students will be suggesting and contributing and creating additional content resources.

5. *Assessment is continuous.* Assessment in onl
   courses is continuous, multiphased and often
   community based rather than concentrated,
   monitored, and primarily individual (Moallem, 2005).
   This is pedagogically beneficial and makes cheating
   and other forms of fraud more difficult. In other
   words, continuous assessment means that you get to
   know the students and students get to know other
   students. Assessment in online courses is also more
   varied, using low-stakes automated quizzes; frequent,
   regular postings in discussion forums; short papers;
   case studies and scenario building; and customizable
   projects. This means redesigning course assessment
   plans. Effective assessment in online courses requires
   getting to know learners as individuals and investing
   more time in coaching and mentoring. The good
   news is that most online course assessments are not
   closed book tests thus do not require proctoring,
   eliminating a whole range of potential challenges
   (Boettcher & Conrad, 2010).

The obstacle of time is one not to be taken lightly as you
prepare to teach an online course. Brookfield (2006) writes,

> *One of the greatest misconceptions about online teaching is
> that it is somehow a "quick and dirty" version of the much
> more complex reality of classroom teaching. Nothing could
> be further from the truth. Teachers who have taught
> online will usually say that their face-to-face classrooms are
> far less time-consuming* . (p. 191)

Find Your Comfort Zone

I enjoy technology as much as anyone but it takes a special
talent to keep up with so many changes. It might take some practice
to realize how the overhead projection system is tied to the computer
and actually how some things work, but it is important to know. I
took several computer classes a few years ago and at the time I felt a
sense of power because I was up-to-date on the latest techniques and
technology. Unfortunately, I do not feel as powerful these days.
You know as well as I do that it seems there is a software update or

new technology every week. Find your comfort zone and if you're not comfortable teaching online classes then let someone else do it. I have fundamental reservations about teaching online. I went through the training and then declined to offer online classes. I have seen horror stories about, for instance, a server going down and throwing the whole class in turmoil. First, I am not sure who is taking the course (or who is on the other end of the computer) and second, I fear learning suffers because even though chat rooms are available, there may not be much interaction. Lastly, I fear for the teacher who has taught too many semesters online and simply gives out reading assignments and exams with little thought to quality. If they are done right, then online courses can be effective learning tools. The preparation time and hours needed to teach online were a bit too much for me so I opted to teach in the classroom. It seems several years ago that many colleges jumped on the bandwagon because so many online universities were extolling the virtues of "going to college in your pajamas." So, in order to compete, mainline colleges and universities started offering online courses. It is a way to increase enrollment and reach previously unreachable students. Like I said, if done right, it can be effective. It was just not my style to teach online. Plus, some courses seem better suited to teaching online than others. Principles of Management and Principles of Marketing would fit well with online offerings, but in teaching Human Relations, I want to be in the classroom face-to-face with students. It boils down to finding your comfort zone. If you do not feel comfortable with some technology then update the skills necessary until you do feel comfortable. An uncomfortable teacher makes for an uncomfortable classroom experience for both student and teacher.

Summary

In summary, online course offerings are here to stay so we must adjust accordingly. My reservations about online teaching include the low completer rate of courses (my online colleagues have much higher drop rates than the classroom courses) and wondering if that's the actual student on the other end of the computer. It is amazing how technology has opened up educational opportunities to so many students because of the distance/convenience factor and online teaching is another valuable tool to be used for learning.

CHAPTER 11

TEACHING STYLE

The Spice of Variety

For the most part, a routine is effective because students know what to expect and that gives them a security blanket. In teaching; however, variety is needed because of different student learning styles. Mixing lectures with application, group discussion, and videos helps different learning styles learn material better. To hearken back to Quintilian (1969) and learning styles, time constraints of the semester make it difficult to ascertain each student's learning style so you will probably teach to the middle of the class with some variety thrown in to hopefully reach the entire class.

Researchers have identified faculty behaviors that set a negative tone for students and affect their academic and intellectual development (Braxton et al., 2004; Buttner, 2004):

- *Inadequate preparation*: failure to order required texts or readers in a timely fashion; inadequate communication about due dates for assignments or about policies on missed or makeup exams; incomplete syllabus.
- *Poor in-class interactions with students*: treating students in a condescending, insensitive, or demeaning manner; putting students down in front of classmates; ignoring students' perspectives; lack of respect for students as individuals.
- *Lack of integrity*: grading students' work on criteria other than merit; treating students unfairly.
- *Failure to provide help*: ignoring students' questions or reacting angrily or defensively when challenged; refusing to provide assistance with assignments.
- *Repeatedly arriving late, running overtime, or ending class early.*

During reviews for exams, I usually write the review on the board so the student will have to copy it. Just the other day I had a student ask me why I didn't type up a handout for the review. I told her that writing on the board forces the student to copy it down so that they are already reviewing for the exam while they are writing. It begins the learning process sooner rather than giving a handout where they are looking in the textbook for answers the night before the exam. I try to think ahead and even if they do not have time to study, or forget there is an exam, just maybe they will remember some of the review from writing it down. I do sometimes use handouts for exam reviews simply because of limited class time.

We all know lectures can be boring, and when I am about to fall asleep during my own lecture it is time to change things up. I have always mixed humor with lectures because if you can make people laugh, you can make them listen. Think back to the most boring professors you had and keep that in mind as you focus on finding your own teaching style. You need to do something that is best for your style and it will probably be best for your students.

There were some courses in graduate school that I really resented. It seemed one professor I had was just marking time until retirement. Class consisted of listening to his boring lectures, taking notes (to help myself stay awake), reading the assigned chapters, and spitting back the information on exam day. On the flip side, I remember as an undergraduate a history professor who reenacted historical scenes and he mesmerized students because we sat on the edge of our seats waiting to see what would happen next. He made learning fun and I actually wanted to go to the library and research historical events. This was a major breakthrough for me because I had always viewed history as a very mundane subject, but when Dr. Reese simply presented the material differently it lit a fire within me that carried over to other subjects as well. It is readily evident to students whether the professor genuinely likes and is enthusiastic about the subject matter because it becomes infectious for the entire class. Thank you, Dr. Reese!!

Teachers could easily be compared to stage actors. If you forget your lines or are not prepared, the audience (class) will know. We must hold their attention and the boring lecture with no student participation is not effective anymore, I'm not sure it ever was. Certainly in any career you will bring some personal/family issues to work, but in teaching it seems more magnified because you must put on the happy face, overcome the bad mood, and get into teaching mode. Students pick up on attitudes very quickly and we must set a positive classroom tone.

Socratic Method

Frequently used as a teaching method in higher education is the Socratic system, which employs the use of questions "to develop a latent idea, as in the mind of a pupil, or to elicit admissions, as from an opponent tending to establish or to confute some proposition." Socrates tended to use his method as his one and only approach to learning; it could be so used today in some cases, but more it is used for variety at the conclusion of lectures, its purpose being to challenge students to think for themselves and, perhaps, reach their own conclusions. The Socratic method suggests that the teacher does the questioning and the student the answering, it also suggests that the teacher answer a student's question with a question of his own. In essence, the student is supposed to find the answer to his/her own question by gaining insight into the facts through provocative questions by the instructor. It would seem that any question-answer period, whether Socratic or otherwise, is a necessary part of any instructor's methods of teaching. Students become frustrated if they do not have the opportunity to ask questions in a class. They have many problems arising out of the learning environment and these problems must be solved if the learning is to be effective. Student questions provide a change of pace, introducing a voice other than the instructor's. As a side effect, the questions allow the student to develop his/her ability to phrase inquiries and present them before a group. A question-answer period serves as a catalyst in soliciting both classroom participation and achievement. Students are apt to be better prepared in their reading and listening assignments if they know they may be challenged or called upon to speak (Kelley & Wilbur, 1970).

We would do well to remember that a teacher is one of the most important adults in a student's life. When implementing rules, procedures, and consequences, all essential to a well-organized learning community, psychologist and teacher Haim Ginott (1972) reminds us to carefully consider and model the behavior we would like to see in our students:

> *I am the decisive element in the classroom. It's my*
> *personal approach that creates the climate. It's my*

daily mood that makes the weather. As a teacher, I possess a tremendous power to make a student's life miserable or joyous. I can be a tool of torture or an instrument of inspiration. I can humiliate or humor, hurt or heal. In all situations it is my response that decides whether a crisis will be escalated and a student humanized or de-humanized. (13)

Grading

Grading is, of course, everything, and it is no surprise that the role of grades in education has been intensely debated; like many other debates, values and ideologies are important (Fowler, 2000). Some scholars view low grades as discouraging students and frustrating their academic progress (Kohn, 1992). Others suggest that it is a distorting, harsh, and punitive practice. Still others are concerned that grades obstruct the improvement of education and hinder at-risk students (Hargis, 1990), thus having undesirable consequences: "grading . . . forecloses on the hopes and aspirations for many students and cosigns them to lower academic ranks, less social status, and reduced employment possibilities before their potential has had a chance to manifest itself" (Edwards, 2000, p. 543).

On the other hand, numerous researchers find that grades have a proper role in the educational process. According to Walvoord and Anderson (1998), "Despite all its problems, grading is still a deeply entrenched mode of evaluating student learning in higher education. It is the basis of a college or university's decision about who graduates. It is the most universal form of communication to employers or graduate schools about the quality of a student's learning" (p. xv). Therefore, grades and grading practices serve important educational and social purposes if used properly.

I do hope the "bell curve" grading system is long gone but I fear some instructors still use it (probably at both the university and community college level). Many of my undergraduate courses were graded on the "bell curve," which is a model that says, for instance, roughly 10% of students get A's, 20% B's, 40% C's, 20% D's, and 10% F's (hence, shaped like a bell). That is so unfair to the student because it espouses competition for the best grades.

Curve systems place students in competition with one another for grades. This competition has two undesirable consequences. First, it discourages cooperative learning, students helping one another. With respect to learning, it makes perfectly good sense that a student who is learning faster or understands better can aid another student to learn course material. Students of roughly comparable ability can help one another in many ways, through discussions of course material as well as cooperative informal testing sessions in which students can sharpen their knowledge. Although competitive grading does not rule out such help, it does discourage it. Second, curve grading reduces students' control over their outcomes because their grades depend not only on how well they perform but also on how others perform. It is considered desirable for students to develop an internal locus of control, the belief that their outcomes depend on their efforts, rather than on luck or immutable abilities. Tying grades to what others do discourages such development (Dominowski, 2002). Will a student help another? Probably not, because he or she could get a higher grade and knock you down to a lower grade. I believe that the instructor should know the material well enough to know what students can and cannot handle. If the exams reflect that, then the "bell curve" is a moot point. I adjust my tests accordingly and if everyone performs to that level then they deserve the higher grade. My philosophy is to start out a little tougher and then ease up as the semester progresses. I think of it as a natural culling to see if students are determined to stay in class and study harder. Those who stay the course are usually rewarded in the end. Also, since we are required to take attendance at a community college, a percentage of the overall grade includes attendance. Of course, that's my choice; you may choose not to do that.

Finally, securing student attention is not just a good idea; it is also essential to learning. Well-placed classroom humor differs from simply telling jokes. Rather, classroom humor is aimed at putting a positive, amusing spin on the lesson content, inviting students to pause, reflect, and process concepts connected with playful laughter. Humor creates a congenial and relaxed classroom atmosphere. More important, cleverly crafted humor facilitates student retention to a greater extent than does the same lesson without added humor (Garner, 2005; Pollak & Freda, 1997).

Strive to Improve

Teaching improvement is something that should go on all the time for all academics. You incorporate a better example or analogy into your lectures, you decide to teach an innovative course or introduce IT in a dynamic way to your discipline. Frequently these changes and improvements are unconscious. However, it is important to become conscious of how and why you change your teaching strategies and methods. There comes a time when change becomes or needs to become deliberative. What is important is to recognize the need for change and develop your teaching. This can be done in investing in peer observation, critical reflection and a conscious change in approach.

In order to change and become aware of the changes you have to distance yourself as a teacher. Teaching is often considered a very insular and private affair. Often as individuals we are willing to let our colleagues critically review our writing and research, yet we are far more hesitant in allowing our peers to review our teaching in action. Even teachers who ask for peer observation are hesitant and defensive when they hear anything negative about their teaching. Of course, it hits too close to home! Distancing yourself allows you to recognize what teaching skills you have and which skills you may still need to develop and attain.

Whatever steps you take to improve or further develop your teaching skills will benefit both yourself and your students' learning. Good effective teaching is very rewarding both personally and professionally. Students appreciate good teaching, which is often reflected in good work and high attendance (Nicholls, 2002).

My dissertation was over student and teacher perceptions in the classroom. No matter how great you think your teaching was for that class period, if students leave scratching their heads and wondering what you were talking about then there was no learning taking place. I'm not sure there is any teaching taking place either. I remember having a statistics professor in college who wrote statistics all over the blackboard the first week of class, but couldn't relate to us (the students). I promptly dropped the class and took it with another professor the following semester. The first professor was impressive but couldn't see that half the class didn't understand. It is all about perception!

Your Credibility

Students define *credibility* as the perception that the teacher has something important to offer and that whatever this "something" is (skills, knowledge, insight, wisdom, information) learning it will benefit the student considerably. Credible teachers are seen as teachers who are worth sticking around because students might learn something valuable from them. They are seen as possessing a breadth of knowledge, depth of insight, sophistication of understanding, and length of experience that far exceeds the student's own. *Authenticity*, on the other hand, is defined as the perception that the teacher is being open and honest in his or her attempts to help students learn. Authentic teachers do not go behind students' backs, keep agendas private, or double-cross learners by dropping a new evaluative criterion or assignment into a course halfway through the semester. An authentic teacher is one that students trust to be honest and helpful. They are seen as flesh and blood human beings with passions, enthusiasms, frailties, and emotions, not as someone who hides behind a collection of learned role behaviors appropriate to the title "professor." From a student's viewpoint both credibility and authenticity need to be recognized in a teacher if that person is to be seen as an important enhancer of learning—as an authoritative ally, in other words (Brookfield, 2006).

In communicating with students, it is not always obvious to them that teachers have a defined area of academic expertise within their own discipline. Therefore, they tend to make inappropriate requests for help on academic matters. Each of us is a specialist in a given area and it is important to let students know exactly where we are prepared to advise and where other colleagues should be consulted (Cox & Heames, 1999).

Group Work

Let's discuss group work briefly. It seems everyone I know, especially students, despise group work where everyone gets the same grade in the group. I have also had unpleasant group experiences, both at work and in school, but it provided a very valuable lesson. The odds are you'll be doing more than your fair share of work because someone will be a slacker or have an excuse for not doing their part for the group. Accept it! I tell my students that when they accept that fact of life, the project will be easier to complete. So often when you have to carry the brunt of the workload, you will be noticed, sooner or later, and your effort will be rewarded. A bit of advice here: try to give students as much class time as possible to work in their groups. It is very difficult for some people to meet outside of class due to work/home demands. Also when you provide class time it takes away any excuses for the work not being done. When everyone in the group receives the same grade they communicate more with each other to make sure they come up with quality results. I am a firm believer in group work and recommend it if your class schedule permits enough time for group projects and teamwork.

Evaluation As a Tool

I am currently working on a peer evaluation where different faculty would visit classrooms at various times within a several week period. To begin with, the opportunity merely to observe others teach and to discuss their approach and your own in detail afterwards can be a rich opportunity for learning. Of course, this would be strictly voluntary and have no bearing on raises, tenure, or end-of-year performance appraisals. It would simply be a tool for improvement, if the teacher was willing to take the risk of having their teaching evaluated. I plan to have various categories, such as: punctuality, student-teacher interaction, lesson application, and so on. The goal is to maximize objectivity and minimize subjectivity in the review process and to make it as complete a picture as possible of the teacher's ability. It might, at some point, be necessary to make the review mandatory, if there are student complaints about the teacher or if the department chair believes it would assist the teacher in reflection and how to improve.

So, in setting up such a review process, I might (as a teacher) have the choice of what days I would like my classroom teaching evaluated. An evaluation during a scheduled exam day would do no one any good. The teacher or the department chair would choose three colleagues for the peer review. They would simply observe a pre-scheduled class period and then rate the various categories on the review sheet. Each faculty member would be responsible for typing up the evaluation and turning it in to the department chair, who would relay that to the appropriate faculty member. This way it is more less anonymous and minimizes risks of any vendettas or hurt feelings. We all want to improve, but it is hard to put your livelihood on the line in front of peers for fear of negative criticism. However, if we don't take the risk in leaving our comfort zone, we can never improve our teaching styles and teach students to the best of our abilities.

Summary
In summary, teaching style revolves around your comfort zone, especially at the beginning of your teaching career. Teach to what you are comfortable with and later on challenge yourself to get a bit "uncomfortable" by modifying teaching styles. Many times the subject matter will dictate a certain teaching style but the key is to always be open to change and to teaching students at their level. You will be more enthusiastic and your students will learn better.

CHAPTER 12

MOTIVATION CHALLENGE

The first few years I was teaching, my skills were up-to-date. While you generally stay abreast of business changes/trends by using the textbook it is imperative to do additional research. We owe it to the students to teach them the very latest and when I am going to the library, watching the national and local news, and reading the Wall Street Journal then I feel that I am more prepared to teach. I mentioned earlier about the importance of staying motivated to do our best and it is an easy trap to fall into by thinking that you have the subject matter down so you need not do anything extra. Wrong! Students know if you are thoroughly prepared or just skimming by.

Sure, you can teach your classes, keep nominal office hours, and then go home, and I have seen instructors do just that. If you are not excited about your subject matter, about the students, and about helping students deal better with this world, then find another career.

Two years after I started teaching, I went back to graduate school to complete my Speech hours so that I could teach Speech and expand my repertoire. I also took a couple of Education courses and I liked the college of Education so much that I decided to stay and work on my doctorate, though my Bachelor's and Master's degrees were in Business. My professors inspired me to continue learning and I really enjoyed the challenging, yet caring atmosphere in the college of Education at Texas Tech University.

The more that I examine motivation, I am not sure that there can be much external motivation where teaching is concerned. It seems that if the fire does not burn from within, then a lit match on the outside will do little good. This is not the easy job everyone thinks it is. For example, I love the Beatles music and I noticed when George Harrison plays the lead that it looks effortless, he smiles, harmonizes, and seldom looks at his guitar. I tried playing that way. Big mistake!! About all I got down pat was the smiling part. Imagine the countless hours George spent practicing, fine tuning, and molding his craft before any fame came his way. It seems the great ones make whatever they do look easy and the same holds true with good teachers. It may look effortless but no one sees the behind-the-scenes hours of preparation that make it look that way. But isn't it worth it when you know a student has grasped a concept? In fact, I always say that I'm going to school, rather than to work. Teaching has never seemed like work to me.

Okay, so far we've discussed self or internal motivation and while I believe that certain external factors can motivate us in the short-term (i.e., pay raise, compliment), there still has to be that desire from within that keeps the drive alive. Do you simply like what you're doing?

I challenge you to continue learning, whether it is through another graduate course, a seminar, or doing independent research. Constantly try to improve your teaching style and getting through to more students. If you are bored about your subject matter, think how your students feel!!

Faculty Complaints

In a study done by Kelley & Wilbur (1970), they listed the top things faculty like *least* about teaching in a community college. I'll list the top five and give my own perspective on them.

1. *Inadequate Working Loads, Compensations, and Aids*. Comments: "The teaching load discourages independent study, professional development, and publication." "Too many clock hours with students." "Salaries are much too low compared to others with less education." "Demands upon time, leaving little time for personal study or family." "Too many committees." "Too many meetings for too few problems." Too many club activities." "Lack of supplies and equipment." "Monotonous, uninteresting duties apart from teaching." "I have too many students and too many classes to do the best job of which I'm capable."

My perspective: Note: It would be very easy to look at all five things faculty like *least* and tell them to toughen up, or that they knew what they were getting in to when they took the teaching job. However, these are legitimate concerns that many faculty have. In addressing workload, my normal workload is teaching 15 hours a week and keeping 8-10 office hours a week. We are required to be on campus the other hours to equal a 35-40 hour work week. I don't see that there's a real problem with having enough hours to do independent study or professional development, if one so chooses. As far as compensation matters, we know what the salary is when we're hired, plus many faculty can choose to teach summer for extra compensation, so complaints of low salaries shouldn't be an issue.

2. *Too Much Diversity and Poor Quality of Students.* Comments: "Frustration of handling lower ability students." "Failure to 'get through' to many students." "Poor quality of majority of students." "We are expected to teach the unteachable in many instances." "Need for working with more talented students." "Students often too immature scholastically." "Tragically poor preparation students get in high school." "Indifference of students toward aims and goals--their satisfaction in just getting by." "Students not taking their work seriously enough." "How to maintain standards with so many poor caliber of students." "Reluctance of some students to accept two-year or terminal programs; many want four years because of draft and unemployment."

My perspective: Diversity and quality of students will always be a community college teaching challenge. The nature of our mission is open access so the biggest challenge will be to maintain high standards for lower performing students who may have little or no knowledge of study skills. Each class will have high and low performing students, but it's our job to teach to both levels. Nobody ever said it was going to be easy, but it's certainly worthwhile.

3. *Loss of Students--Limitations of Two-Year College.* Comments: Lack of graduate student--most frustrating." "Cannot keep students long enough to watch and help them grow." "Losing students so fast." "Students leave just when we get to know them." "Students miss influence of juniors and seniors to set standards of excellence."

My perspective: Loss of students and limitations of attending only two years is out of our control. Teach the students to the best of your ability and help them grow and mature in the short time they attend. When we encourage and give them the basic learning tools it will sustain them for a lifetime.

4. *Poor Status, Prestige, and Influence of the Community College.* Comments: "Attitudes of some four-year college people to which our students transfer." "The idea that one is less able or competent in his subject than his colleagues at the four-year college or university." "Does not have the university image." "No rank

among our faculty, while university people enjoy this extra status symbol." "External factors--lack of recognition of the roll of our school in higher education."

My perspective: Poor status and prestige continue to be problems at the community college level and it seems many sitcoms pick up on the less than average son or daughter having to go to a community college because they couldn't get into a university. Community colleges are easy fodder for comedians and much of the status and prestige is out of our control but we can slowly work toward gaining more respect by fulfilling our mission in the community. Some university faculty look down on community college faculty because we aren't under the gun to publish and do research, we only teach. I think in many ways that is to our advantage, but we must also do independent study to keep our teaching skills honed to the highest level. It was a huge compliment to community colleges when my graduate school professor admitted she couldn't do my job because she went straight through school and into teaching, which is for teaching academic subjects (English, Math, History, and so on). In teaching Business classes, one must have actual real world work experience to apply the learned theories/concepts to reality.

5. *Administrative faults (personnel, policies, attitudes)*. Comments: "High school attitudes of the administration." "Administrative failures, such as in registration policies." "Poor communication with the administration, who know little of the community college." "Lack of voice in policy making." "Weak, untrained administrators." "Administrators who reward mediocrity and ignore merit in teaching."

My perspective: I've not had any problems with administrative faults and attitudes. Most administrators understand our teaching challenges and assist when needed. They know we are all working towards the same goal and if, for example, there's an issue with registration then administrators work to get the problem resolved.

Motivating Students

Now, how do we motivate students?? We must take a multi-faceted approach. First, we need students to see us teaching enthusiastically and in a dedicated manner. We don't need to visit

Maslow or Herzberg at this point in our discussion on motivation but be aware that some students may lack the funds to even buy a book and if those basic needs are not met then the student has little chance of success. Second, we need to give timely feedback which means grading tests as quickly as possible and letting students know their standing in the class. Third, being professional, caring individuals, helps students realize a quality education and presents a good role model. Finally, getting involved with students and listening to them will pay dividends because they will try harder when they view you as a coach and guide, rather than as an unapproachable adversary. All of this will trigger their internal motivation to want to continue their education and to succeed.

How Do You View Your Students?

At this point, it's important to look at leadership styles because they have a bearing on how well students are motivated to learn. McGregor's Theory X and Theory Y remind us that each supervisor manages employees according to his or her own attitudes and ideas about people's needs and motivations. Following are the basic assumptions of McGregor's Theory X and Theory Y (McGregor, 1960).

Theory X: *The assumption that most employees dislike work, avoid responsibility, and must be coerced to work hard.*

Theory Y: *The assumption that most employees enjoy work, seek responsibility, and can self-direct.*

These theories have great implications for teachers. If a teacher views the student from Theory X, then the teacher is more likely to think the student is lazy, is never prepared, and some form of punishment is put in place (i.e., attendance penalties) to keep the student in line.

On the other hand, the Theory Y teacher will view students from a more positive perspective, give them challenging assignments, and assume they are motivated to learn. Remember, the Pygmalion effect? We do tend to live up to others' expectations and that would certainly be apropos in the classroom.

What is important to appreciate is that students adapt to the requirements they perceive teachers expect of them. They usually try to please their teachers, and they do what they think will bring them rewards within the system. The context that is set for teaching depends on the following elements:

- *the curriculum that is taught;*
- *the teaching methods selected;*
- *the assessment procedures selected;*
- *the feedback procedure implemented;*
- *the climate created between teacher and student;*
- *institutional expectations, rules and regulations* (Biggs, 1999).

The student's interest in the subject matter of the task is a crucial element of the deep approach to learning, as is the individual teacher. The attitudes and enthusiasm of a teacher, his or her concern for helping the students understand, and particularly his or her ability to understand the difficulties experienced by students in dealing with a new topic, will all affect the learning approaches adopted by the student.

A Balancing Act

The difficulty for the lecturer is to obtain a balance, allowing for sufficient flexibility for the support of individual learning but also maintaining a structure where a whole group of students can be kept on track and allowed to learn and develop through a course, module or entire program. Student autonomy and self-directed learning supported by the teacher would seem to be an encouraging step forward. What the teacher should be looking for is to move beyond the enhancement of student performance within a narrow spectrum of learning activities and teaching situations and the development of foundation skills, such as self-directed learning and learning autonomy (Nicholls, 2002).

Staying motivated to do your best job is a challenge in any line of work. Teachers who remain passionate about teaching experience a high degree of professional satisfaction. Huberman (1993) described four necessary conditions for such satisfaction:

a. *an enduring commitment to the profession after being appointed with tenure;*

b. *'manageable' classes, and where one can maintain good relations with students;*

c.   *good relationships with colleagues; and*
d.   *a balance between school and home life/personal interests.*

These four conditions for professional satisfaction are crucial. Certainly tenure helps the passion, but shouldn't you feel the commitment and passion even before being granted tenure? I agree wholeheartedly about maintaining good relations with students and colleagues. Who would want to work someplace where they dread having to deal with coworkers or customers? Of course, there will be times when a troublesome student or situation will cause some consternation but overall good relations manifest themselves in being motivated and excited about teaching. Finally, it is very important to have balance in one's life. When you have a healthy support system and interests outside of the classroom it makes you a more complete individual and teacher. You are better able to relate teaching to the real world and maintain self-motivation.

John Ruskin (1851) said:

> *In order that people may be happy in their work, these three things are needed: they must be fit for it; they must not do too much of it; and they must have a sense of success in it.*

Summary

In summary, we've discussed the importance of self-motivation and its importance to teaching and making a difference in students' lives. There will always be faculty complaints about workload, student quality, and the administration, but it simply comes down to knowing that any career choice will have challenges. I mentioned that my job never seems like work because I enjoy what I do. Finally, how you view students will determine your teaching success. Expect much, receive much! (Pygmalion effect) On the other hand, if you expect little and give up easily on student challenges then you will not find teaching very fulfilling.

CHAPTER 13

CHAIRPERSON

Have you ever worked in a day care center? If you have, then you will be well-prepared to be department chair. I am joking, of course, but sometimes it seems that way. I had the opportunity to be chairperson after I finished my doctorate and came very close to accepting the position. Of course, becoming a department chair initially concerned me because I teach morning and evening classes and feared I would be here 12 to 14 hours-a-day. I thought about how many meetings I would be attending and that many times I would have to drop what I was doing to attend to a problem and decided I would be more effective staying in the classroom full-time. I turned down the department chairperson position when it was offered to me because I preferred the classroom to meetings or typing up reports. This was a personal choice and is certainly not an indictment of the position, it was just not for me. We need both faculty and administration to be a successful educational institution so move towards what you enjoy and the area in which you feel you can contribute most. On a side note, I still remember my niece attending my doctoral celebration and saying "Uncle Jimmy, now you can be the college president!" (that sounded nice but not hardly)

Being offered the department chair position was an honor and also a trigger event in my life because I had aspirations to move up into administration as far as possible, but I decided I would miss the students too much. I also felt that I was not very effective sitting in meetings. I preferred to be on the front lines where the action is, so to speak. At that point, I defined what I wanted to do as far as my teaching career goes. I was happy with that direction, and I still am.

Chairperson Responsibilities

A study of supervisors, chairpersons, and faculty at Delaware Technical and Community College (Winner, 1989) found all three groups agreeing that the chairs had major responsibility for identifying departmental personnel needs, evaluating the staff, establishing departmental curricular goals, evaluating instructional materials, and representing the department to the administration and the public.

Hammons (1984), who has studied department chairs extensively, reviewed a great number of studies of chairperson responsibilities and activities and identified at least forty different functions categorized under five major headings: administration, student oriented, business and financial, faculty oriented, and curriculum and instruction. Finding a major problem to be that few of the chairs had received any preservice assistance in learning what their responsibilities were or how to fulfill them, he concluded that the role of the chair is among the most nebulous in the institution. Numerous responsibilities, most of them vaguely worded, are assigned, but few opportunities to learn how to manage them are provided. Portolan (1992) confirmed that the instructional administrators she studied seemed to be experiencing a middle management syndrome of feeling ineffective and powerless. Faced with changing student populations, limited resources, and a range of faculty issues they had not been prepared to handle, they were developing feelings of alienation toward their work.

The duties of a department chair vary widely from institution to institution. The chair is the person who must keep the whole department running and also supervises the support and secretarial staff.

Department chairs are in charge of programs. This may include completing class schedules and ensuring that all classes are offered when needed. They write and submit reports to provost and presidents regarding majors and minors, and they are charged with keeping professional programs accredited. This involves attendance at conferences and ongoing training from the accrediting agencies, such as ones in education, nursing, or business. The reports and paperwork can be tremendous.

Department chairs work one-on-one with students. They are often the judge for letting students register late for a full class, or for allowing a student to switch sections. They hear student complaints.

Budgets constitute a huge part of a department chair's duties. Supplies, equipment, and travel monies for faculty are increasingly expensive and budgets are rarely limitless.

<u>Why Be a Department Chair?</u>
Why do people accept the duties of being a department chair? Many professors become chairs because they believe in the service

aspect of the position. Chairs can be advocates for people and programs, and chairs can get things done that support improvements for students. Many people accept a chair position as a stepping stone to a future administrative position—a deanship. Others take on the chair's duties because of increased pay (Clement, 2010).

At our college we have had some trying moments with our dress code policy. Many faculty believe that we are role models for students and that we should dress professionally (the older generation, or, my generation). However, there is another group that feels we are teaching a subject and that it should not matter what we wear. After conflicting signals from administration it has been decided, informally, that we should dress to our own standards. I can certainly see both sides of the issue but still feel strongly that we should be representatives of our profession and dress accordingly, especially in the business department. This might be one of the myriad of problems you would have to deal with as department chair.

After you become a community college teacher, you might aspire to move up into administration. Please know that you are dealing with many egos and they can clash at times. It seems one faculty member wants one thing and then someone wants something else. And sometimes faculty get upset because they think the chair is playing favorites. As in any office setting, I believe you have an advantage if you play politics well. But I believe the key is to be a team player and try to get along with others. It goes a long way in determining your success.

A Real-Life Scenario

The following scenario is not meant to dissuade you from aspiring to be a department chair but a dose of reality is always good for the soul. As department chair, you will probably have to deal with similar situations.

This is about three faculty members that I will refer to as the "three pistols." This group of individuals is out of ammunition but they keep firing anyway. These faculty members, or "pistols," have, at separate times, written to our college president (a huge no-no) over various issues. This is a group that really has no clue about the concepts of chain of command, proper communication, or commitment.

"Derringer," wrote complaining about our department chair, "Colt," wrote asking for a raise, and "Revolver," wrote with complaints in general. They did not follow the chain of command, which I teach in Principles of Management and they should have known better anyway if they had ever held another job. Of course, our president reminded "Derringer" and "Revolver" that there is a protocol for registering complaints. They should first meet with the department chair, then proceed to the next level, which would be the dean. "Colt" met with the president, at the president's request, and was told in no uncertain terms that if he was not happy with his salary that he could leave at any time and seek employment elsewhere. "Colt" is still here.

"Revolver" tried to condense a 10 week summer course into 5 weeks. Many students complained and he got into trouble for that. Once the schedule is set, faculty cannot change meeting times or days. It's a no brainer. Students take classes to fit their daily schedules and it is not fair or appropriate, not to mention against policy, to change that once classes have begun.

"Derringer" has several degrees, no common sense, and is very susceptible to other colleague's opinions. The three pistols are never happy and also gripe about what they perceive as unfairness regarding teaching load. They remind me of a run I took once with a small, yipping dog at my heels trying to constantly nip me. They are always there and ready to nit-pick the smallest perceived injustice. Without going into specifics, suffice it to say, they affect the morale of our department.

Do you still want to be department chair? Our department chair has meetings, planned and spur-of-the-moment, and helps interpret policy from upper-level administration so we can do our jobs properly. But, he also has to deal with continuing personnel issues. The "three pistols," are perfect examples of what you might face. Also, there are budgets to be presented and okayed, which is another requirement of the department chairs position. I respect my department chair and he has performed well in his leadership role. I admire department chairs a great deal and I wish you the best if you choose to climb the community college ladder!

Summary

In summary, the department chair position carries with it a great deal of responsibility. The chair is not only responsible for day-to-day duties such as budgets, class schedules, handling student complaints, holding meetings to disseminate information to faculty, to name a few, but must also contend with faculty and staff egos. I would think it's a very challenging, yet rewarding career move and one that can build many ties and friendships. Please be aware of the responsibilities of the position because in the process you basically become a first-line supervisor, or assembly line foreman, to put it in business vernacular.

CHAPTER 14

INTO THE SEMESTER: MY DIARY

Here is a brief diary of a typical semester that you may find helpful:

Weeks 1-4

Develop your syllabus. The teaching methods by which the course will be taught, the assessment methods by which the students will be assessed and the evaluation methods by which the course will be reviewed and improved, all play an essential role in course design. This is particularly the case in terms of their alignment. Unaligned and/or reproductively aligned courses can be particularly detrimental to the development of deeper and richer learning experiences. Course objectives, course content and course structures may, for example, convey a great deal about a course to the student. How the course engages them, how it is assessed and even to some degree how it is evaluated are, however, much more revealing. These are fundamental to developing a complete syllabus (Light, Cox, & Calkins, 2009).

You will be given a basic format, but you will also have some leeway in developing your syllabus.   It is of paramount importance to include detailed information in your syllabus because you will have to live by it the entire semester. If a student challenges a grade, then you had better have everything delineated in the syllabus for backup. I sometimes use a fudge factor (5% for participation) to reward students who are prepared and participate in class discussion. However, assigning a participation grade taught me a valuable lesson. Case in point, I had a student who participated negatively throughout the semester. He didn't like the room temperature, the lights were too bright, or he didn't like the class exercises. Well, I gave him a low participation grade and he promptly challenged it. He argued that he did participate, albeit negatively. And he was right, so from then on I wrote into my syllabus "participation includes positive contributions to class discussion, attitude, and respect for others." I enjoy sitting down before finals with the roster and seeing who contributed to class most and assigning grades. I have never given below a "C" for participation because even if they sit quietly the entire semester they are forced to participate in projects and class surveys.

Naturally, there will be some required information to put in your syllabus. For instance, your name, the name of the course, office hours, textbook used, attendance/grading policy, and the course schedule. Again, please be careful to make this as detailed as possible because you will have to live by your word. Students will challenge syllabus details at times and if everything is not in black and white, then you may have problems because it is hard to change rules during the semester unless it's in the student's favor. Some teachers also figure a percentage of the course grade for attendance—since the student is required to attend, it makes sense to reward them for their attendance.

As can be seen, a syllabus is a complex document that captures a great deal of thought. It is the students' guide to the course and provides procedural protection for both students and instructors. The syllabus describes how things will be done in a course, and if that is the way they are done, no one has a valid basis for complaint.

Although the emphasis in constructing a syllabus is properly on clear and sufficiently complete description of course components, attention should also be given to visual appearance. Students should be able to easily locate important information, such as test dates and due dates for assignments. Also, it's handy if the syllabus can be contained on one sheet of paper, which seems more feasible by keeping in mind that two-sided printing doubles the capacity of a sheet. If an assignment requires lengthy, detailed instructions, it is best to describe these in a separate document, rather than trying to include them in the syllabus.

The first day of class should be devoted to giving an overview of the course and reviewing the course syllabus, explaining the reasoning that went into designing the course, and answering any questions students might have. Doing so usually takes most of a class period and gives the students an excellent introduction to the course (Dominowski, 2002).

First impressions. If you do not set a positive tone from the get-go, it will be a long semester for you. The old adage that making a positive first impression is much easier than attempting to overcome a negative first impression is so true! Most people assess another person very quickly and then settle on a general perception of that individual. Research conducted at Carleton University in Ottawa indicates that people are registering likes and dislikes in as little as 1/20th of a second (Zaslow, 2006). Everyone is nervous with anticipation the first day of class and that is to be expected. Being friendly, approachable, and understanding will start the class off well. I find a bit of humor to be an excellent ice breaker and it tends to put the students at ease. When they smile or laugh, their ears open up and they are amenable to listening.

Our college is supported by state funds on the basis of attendance reports, so it is imperative to keep accurate attendance records for class. Students on financial aid who drop out after receiving their checks at certain points during the semester are required to pay back the funds. The college can be held liable for paying back those funds if the student attempts to cheat the system. Since we are required to take attendance, I correlate names with faces as quickly as possible. The moment I call roll and ask them if they would prefer to be called by a nickname, I work very hard beginning to learn names. I have always felt that knowing a student's name goes a long way towards building a relationship because it shows that the student is important to you. I always impress when I call each of my 32 students by name at the end of the first class meeting. I usually relay to them; however, that I will forget again because I have other classes to meet and names will start running together. I average 125 students per semester. But making an attempt to learn names shows you care about them as individuals. I had a Math instructor friend who used a seating chart and never took the time to learn names. He said names were of little importance and that they were there to learn math. He is right, but I disagree! Names are something I constantly work on and I think the students appreciate it. Isn't it just common sense to want to be called by your name? It demonstrates that you are approachable and that you care about them.

Again, negative first impressions are difficult to overcome, but I think it is a bit easier in a classroom setting. The teacher is more likely to overcome a negative first impression with subsequent knowledge/expertise on the subject matter. But making a positive first impression gets the class on track quickly and sets the stage for learning.

Slow is okay. The first week, students are going through the add/drop process and adjusting their schedules, so the first week I go slowly. I concentrate on going over the syllabus, doing introductions, and talking informally to students. In the past, I tried launching into the subject matter enthusiastically the first week only to have several students add the class during late registration, so I basically had to start over. Do whatever is best for you. You will also need to tend to any special needs students. I occasionally have hearing impaired students who need interpreters and someone to take notes, so you will have to work that out as the challenge presents itself. I also am busy inputting students on to the attendance spreadsheet so I will have all of their names and a current roster.

Some of my colleagues have students sign "contracts" at the beginning of the semester. The contract deals with attendance, turning in assignments on time and generally asking for the student's commitment to the course. I have not used them but they sound like a great alternative to get the student started on the right track and committed to completing the course. Many times I will cover a handout of seven ways to help the student succeed. It reads as follows:

SEVEN WAYS TO "ACE" THIS COURSE
(or any course)

1. **Attend!** There is nothing more important than attending. It shows you are trying and that you are disciplined enough to get here, and on time. Will your boss let you show up when you want to? No! You must put forth the effort and showing up helps you do that!

2. **Participate!** With smaller classes it makes it easy to contribute to class discussion. I don't plan to do all of the talking and your opinions matter to me!

3. **Communicate with me!** If you miss class, please let me know. I can't help you if you don't let me. What am I to think when you miss 2 or 3 times and I don't hear from you? Are you sick? Having trouble? Are you dropping? Please be upfront with me because I will be upfront with you.

4.   **Do your assignments!** It is a barometer to me of whether you care about this course. Usually assignments don't count a great deal, EXCEPT when you don't do them. A 5 or 10% reduction can hurt your grade considerably. Why drag your grade average down by not turning them in? It makes no sense.

5.   **Respect your classmates!** You'll learn a great deal from each other and who knows, maybe someone will help you study.

6.   **Read the chapters!** It helps you learn, shows effort, and makes it easier when reviewing material for an exam because you've already gone over it once.

7.   **Listen in class!** So much exam material is taken from class discussion and listening helps you digest the concepts and prepares you well for success! If your neighbor wants to talk then wait until after class or break.

I plan to be here for every class and to be prepared! Will you do the same?

Budgets will be due soon, so you may need to communicate with colleagues as to what will be cut from, or added to the budget. In addition, we are working on SACS recommendations about attempting to assess each course with learning objectives and whether those learning objectives were met by semesters' end. Then we must come up with a plan as to how to improve on the assessment results. Right now, we are in a state of flux because every time we come up with something, it changes and we have to start over. I am trying to bear with it because assessment is a very difficult thing to accomplish in Business. It is not as easy as giving a keyboarding test to see how many words per minute the student can type. This is another way for the community college to justify its existence to the state and to accrediting bodies so we are required to comply. Let's face it, assessment and justifying our existence as a community college are here to stay. It's really nothing new because we do assessments using final exams for the course and various assessments throughout the semester but we simply need to prove to accrediting agencies that we know what we are doing and that students are learning. Many state budgets have cut education funding and as an example of justification, the Texas Higher Education Coordinating Board (THECB) previously required each program to graduate at least 5 students per year with an average of 25 over 5 years. In April, 2012, that changed to 8 graduates per year with an average of 40 over 5 years.

<u>Weeks 5-8</u>

Things are settling in and I am into a routine. I have to put together each round of exams, plus the bookstore needs book orders for summer and next fall.

Book orders. I am thinking of changing publishers because some books are getting too expensive and the student's question me about it. When I first started teaching I always tried to choose the best book for the course and never knew or paid attention to the price. Nowadays, I not only look at content but if the price is not reasonable then I choose a different book. I was under the illusion that a majority of students had grants but have since learned only roughly 50% receive some type of financial aid. That still leaves a lot of students paying their own way or working to be able to buy necessary school materials. Please be industrious when choosing publishers, it seems more and more of them are taking advantage of students. In one class, I have a paperback book that sells for $70, but students cannot sell their book back. Why? Because the publisher prints a new edition <u>every</u> year, so the student gets caught either way. They can either buy the hardbound textbook for $220 and sell it back for $50, or they can buy the paperback for $70 with no buy back. (Excuse me, while I get on my soapbox). I tell my students to get the book the cheapest way they can. If they can get it through Amazon.com, or a digital copy on a reader, or even renting the book, it suits me just fine. Unfortunately, ever since I was an undergraduate nothing much has changed regarding textbook procedures. It is not fair to students. It is up to us, as instructors, to choose the lowest priced, highest quality book possible.

Choosing the right textbook is critical to a successful classroom experience for both the teacher and student. Well-organized texts are both coherent and informationally complete. These two aspects are strongly related to interest in and learning made possible by texts. As texts become less user friendly, or as students become less knowledgeable about text content, teachers should make a greater effort to provide useful background knowledge about the text, given that knowledge and coherence appear to make separate contributions (McKeown et al., 1992). Also, research suggests that text vividness has a positive impact on interest and learning, provided the vivid information is germane to the learning task. Texts that include irrelevant or highly seductive information may actually interfere with learning by diverting readers' attention from important text segments (Harp & Maslich, 2005; Harp & Mayer, 1998).

The textbook for a course should cover a high percentage of the topics deemed important by the instructor, in a manner that is appropriate to the level of the course and compatible with the instructor's approach to course content. The choice of a textbook is influenced by the desired amount of overlap between textbook and lectures. Estimating the difficulty level of a textbook for students is an important but difficult task. Basic measures such as word length and sentence length give some idea of text difficulty. Pedagogical aids such as chapter summaries, clear definitions of new terms, ample use of examples, and relevant illustrations make textbooks easier to understand (Dominowski, 2002).

Bringing in outside material that relays up-to-date information is most helpful and provides real world application for students. Any supplemental material to the textbook can be used and as you progress through the semester you may want to focus on different concepts more than others. I still copy a chapter from a previous edition that was deleted because I feel it is more pertinent to our subject than the new chapter. The textbook is the course guide but tailor the course as needed.

Schedules. We are now turning in our summer and fall class offerings so they can print the appropriate schedule of classes for the students. At this point you may need to meet with colleagues about any time changes to your classes or any new course offerings so you can run trial schedules and make sure class times don't conflict with core courses that students are required to take. I am also dropping the first students who are not attending or have reached their limit on absences. I try to be as lenient as possible due to flu season, family tragedies, and personal problems in general, but I must also be fair to students who attend regularly. When too many absences occur, there simply comes a point where it is best for the student to drop and try again next semester.

Okay, we are half way through the semester, things are smoothing out and students are participating and feeling more confident. We have all gotten over the beginning of the semester jitters, the first couple of exams are complete, and we are settling into a routine. Also, some students are asking for recommendation letters for scholarships and I'm happy to oblige.

Weeks 9-12

This period is probably the best time of the semester for me. I am in teaching mode and making exams, challenging students, and answering questions about various projects they are working on. We now know one another's expectations and that is a good thing. Of course, there is an occasional meeting and I am still working on learning outcomes for the SACS requirements. Also, there is graduation paperwork starting to filter in, so I need to certify that all requirements have been met, whether certificate or degree. Around this time the registrar opens up online registration for the next semester so many students will need advising in the next few weeks. Some teachers post sign-up sheets on their door for advising but I had too many students who would sign up for a time slot and then not show for various reasons. Now I announce to my classes they are welcome to drop by during office hours and we can discuss their schedules. This method seems to work best for me.

Weeks 13-16

We are starting to wrap up the semester and working towards final exams. I sometimes use previous finals but mostly I prepare new exams to better reflect what the class has discussed throughout the semester. I have a philosophy that some people may or may not agree with, but I took many classes where I never even knew where I stood in the class because we never got an exam back until it was too late to drop the course. Or, the final exam was the majority of the grade. I think that is unfair. I return exams the next class period because going over exams is a valuable learning tool and the students receive immediate feedback. My philosophy is to start tougher and ease up toward final exam time. That way, the student builds credits throughout the semester and the course grade does not hinge on one huge, all-encompassing exam at the end counting 50% or more. I am certainly not averse to having comprehensive final exams, especially when there are certain objectives you want the student to take from the course, like Math. You will have your own style but I usually count the final equal to or slightly more than the other exams during the semester, so my finals are generally 20-25% of the overall course grade.

In wrapping up the semester, I must be careful to stay out of my Critical Parent mode. Students want to know what they need to get on the final to, for instance, get a "B" in the course. I tell them 100! I don't know anyone who can study for an 85 on the final so they can get a "B". I always tell them to study hard and go for a 100. Usually during finals week I'll have many students who need advising for the next semester, so I have to juggle that with grading papers. Of course, there are always a couple of students who have emergencies and ask to take the exam at another time. I can usually oblige them, but we do have deadlines to post grades. Most students are able to take the exam within a day of their emergency. This is a very hectic time of the semester and flexibility and patience are key. The Critical Parent mode is not the key!

The semester is over! You have graded all final exams and turned in your grades. I usually return for my office for a day or two for housekeeping, answering student emails, or just simply preparing what I can for the next semester. This relieves some of the pressure about starting a new term because the first few days of reporting back always seem to be the busiest. After the initial euphoria of semester's end, this is where melancholy creeps in. It is a transition to which you will need to adjust. After ramping up energy levels throughout the entire semester, finals mark an abrupt end. It is like going 100 miles-per-hour and then suddenly coming to a stop. This is not meant to scare you and you will not go into a deep, dark depression. But be aware that the body needs some time to adjust. I am usually okay for a couple of days wrapping things up, relaxing, and reflecting on the semester. Then, after a few days I am so lethargic I cannot even seem to move, or care if I do. I have talked to several teachers who experience going through the same cycle. This will pass and you will be back in a routine shortly. I simply want you to be aware that any transition takes some adjustment time.

Summary

In summary, I've taken you through a typical semester from calling roll to posting final grades. Please don't be deterred from teaching after reading the preceding diary because there will be enough time to complete everything. Like any career choicc, there are busy times and not so busy times when one can get caught up. Did I mention when you love what you do that teaching never seems like work?

CHAPTER 15

STORIES/RECOLLECTIONS

Beware, you may experience these or similar situations:

No Pleasing Her

I had a student in my Human Relations class when I was a relatively new instructor and she questioned everything I did. The other students would sit there in shock while she challenged almost everything I said. We were doing an exercise one day when she refused to participate and said it was a high school exercise and she would not do it. I remember her sitting there while the rest of the class discussed it. I dreaded coming to that class because I never knew what problems she would cause that day. I finally told her that if it was so easy that she should get an "A" without much effort. Honestly, it was a battle of wills for the entire semester. I wanted to handle the problem student myself and did not seek much input from the dean or administration. My colleagues said she acted the same way in their classes, which was of little comfort to me. Several years later, after she graduated, she sent me a plant with a note that said "thank you for teaching me humility." I almost fell over! She finally saw the value of what we were doing in class and it almost made all the conflict worthwhile. I will never forget Anna.

Determined Student

Earlier, I was talking about how community college students are different from university students. I had a student come to me just before final exams, crying, and she said her boyfriend had just gotten out of jail and told her she did not need to be in school. He threw her books away and she had no way to study for the exam. I loaned her my book and let her take the final exam late. It was obvious to me that the boyfriend thought she would get educated and leave him. Exactly! I told her that if the boyfriend really cared about her that he would support her endeavors or maybe even attend class with her.

Don't Praise Him

I had a student who showed lots of potential and I was telling my colleagues about him and they told me to be sure to never praise him or he would drop the class. I thought that was so silly. Who does not want positive reinforcement? I praised the student and he never showed up again. Go figure? That will always be a mystery to me.

Preparedness

You will, no doubt, have trying experiences that make you wonder why you even started teaching. I gave a Math exam this morning and 4-5 students showed up more than 5 minutes late and two of them had nothing to write with! How can you show up for an exam, especially Math, and not have a writing utensil?? I told them when we went over the answers the next class period that I have the right to ask them to leave class if they are not prepared and that it was not up to me to supply them with pencils. Scenarios like this really test your patience, so be prepared!

The Stalker

There is certainly a need for administrators in a college setting but personally, I had no use for them in this instance. I try to teach my class to the best of my ability and when a student is out of line or there are problems, I expect to be backed up by administration. I had a female student stalking me and after documenting everything she was doing, per administrative instructions (she was writing me love notes, driving by my house, etc.), she was allowed to stay in class until I caused such a fuss that they had another teacher work with her, relaying my assignments. I requested that she be dropped from my course. She was not and I was really disappointed. I have found that I have to handle and make decisions not in my job description. I truly believe it is because everyone is afraid of lawsuits. It seems that is the way society has become and we have lost a lot of accountability and responsibility in everyday life. I am the first to admit that the classroom is not a democracy. The student has a right to drop the class and take another instructor if he or she cannot live by the rules set forth in the course syllabus (there's the importance of a proper syllabus, again). Allow me to get on my soapbox momentarily, but academic freedom deals with trusting us to teach what we deem necessary for students to learn in the classroom. However, I also think that administrators should totally support faculty and take action when we request it. (okay, I'm off my soapbox, thanks)

Hygiene Issues

I had a student recently who was obviously not college material and had some mental issues as well as personal hygiene issues. He seemed to just be excited to be in college and didn't seem to understand the concept of taking notes or studying for exams. His odor was so pungent that the other students moved away from him, so he was affecting my entire class. Administrators were involved and I finally had to tell the student in no uncertain terms that he had the right to pass or fail my course, but if he smelled bad I would ask him to leave the room. I owe it to all of my students to create an atmosphere conducive to learning. Unfortunately, this was only resolved when the student accumulated enough absences to be dropped from the course.

The Know-It-All

I had a know-it-all student who questioned everything I said and acted like he was too smart for my course. Several weeks passed and I was hoping he would settle into learning but he was getting argumentative in class. One night after class I had a candid discussion with him and told him that if he was so knowledgeable that I would let him present a chapter for class. He loved it and after presenting the chapter he seemed to support me the rest of the semester. We had no problem from then on and I guess he just needed a platform for a brief spotlight moment. My other approach, which I have used one other time with a know-it-all, was to ask them after class why they were taking the course. I get the attitude that if they are so smart, they should be teaching the class. It is a legitimate question and that usually solves the problem.

The Visitor

Sometimes you will have a student that for some reason, thinks they need to constantly drop by your office to "smooze" and shoot the breeze. They will talk about the weather, sports, their job, or really anything, including class. I still haven't figured them out. I guess they think if they visit with the professor that they will get a higher grade. I keep my office hours for when the student needs assistance. I started using a body language technique on him and when he came into my office I would literally turn my back on him and type at the keyboard or act like I was extremely busy—it had no effect! What I considered rude behavior on my part never stopped him. Who knows what students are thinking? I can partially understand such behavior because I believe students want to be friendly and feel good about their collegiate experience. I like enthusiasm for learning so I will visit anytime with someone bettering themselves, but I also like to stay on task. Stopping by an instructor's office for brownie points not only does not help, but can sometimes hurt the student.

The Dominator
This semester I have a student who is trying too hard for participation points. She is in three of my classes back-to-back and it is a challenge to keep her from dominating class discussion. I can usually limit a student from talking too much by asking other students their opinions, but I increasingly find myself speeding up my lecture in hopes she won't interrupt. It's gotten so bad that when I dismiss class I almost race to the door in hopes of leaving before she asks another question. Unfortunately, most of the time I don't make it to the door in time. I do value student input; however, she tends to ask questions I can't answer and seems to simply want to vent her frustrations. The other day she asked why a government agency refused her request for funds and I really could not answer that question. I told her she needed to ask the agency, not me. I hope to learn her motives by the end of the semester because while some students want to just participate, others think the class is a captive audience for their opinions, and still others like to talk to hear themselves.

I'll Do Anything!
We will have students from the local university who come to the community college because they are on probation and need to raise their gpa. However, many have the misconception that the courses will be easier and that they can skate through with an easy "A". One such student had many absences in my class and halfway

through the semester I counseled him to not miss another class or he would lose his attendance grade, which is 10 percent of the course grade (this knocks them down a letter grade but they can still pass the course). Within a week he was absent again and accumulated more absences before the semester ended. He finished the course with a low "D" and came storming into my office for an explanation. He said he would do anything, extra credit, or even another project to raise his grade to a "C". I promptly reminded him of our understanding about his absences and that he continually missed without attempting to contact me or explain why. The grades were already posted and he was so far away from a "C" that extra credit at that point was useless, even if I could change the grade. He was livid and said he would now have to repeat the class. If he does repeat it, I doubt that he'll choose my class.

The 4.0 Students

It seems every semester I have one or two students who explain to me right from the get-go that they have a 4.0 gpa so far and basically expect an "A" in my class also. I simply tell them to prove it in my class and they will earn an "A," rather than politicking for it. This kind of attitude never ceases to amaze me! I guess, after being told that, I should immediately give them an "A" for the semester and tell them they no longer need attend? Yeah, right!

Summary

The preceding scenarios are simply a heads-up about possible issues you may encounter. Each student/class has its own personality and while there will be spotlight seekers there will also be totally quiet students who also need assistance. It is our job to try to reach everyone in the class with minimal disruptions and maximal learning. I'm sure after you teach for a few years that you will have many of your own stories and recollections.

CHAPTER 16

HOW BADLY DO YOU WANT THIS?

There are several factors influencing candidates in search for academic jobs. The seven different factors include: demographics, the general academic job market, cultural diversity, conditions within the discipline, institution-specific issues, politics at one's current institution, and your personal background and assets.

Demographic Trends. Underlying the demand for education at all levels are demographic trends. The baby boom generation expanded higher education phenomenally, but they are now retiring in record numbers. This opens the door for many who want to pursue academics for their vocation.

The State of the General Academic Job Market. In addition to demographic trends, the general academic job market is affected by the state of the economy and the prevailing political climate. The state of the economy is particularly relevant to colleges, because economic conditions directly affect state revenue projections which, in turn, affect state budgets and allocations for higher education. In Texas, we just went through a bone chilling budget cut, but there will always be a need for qualified teachers.

The Need for Cultural Diversity. Most colleges have been under pressure to become more representative of the students they serve and of the overall population. Currently, there is still a need for solid, qualified teachers at the college level, no matter the ethnicity.

Demand for and Conditions Within Your Discipline. Some academic disciplines have a greater demand for faculty than do others. There are usually more job candidates in liberal arts and humanities.

Insitutional Constraints and Politics at the Institution Where You Are Interviewing. Some institutions may be unsure at the start of the academic job market season whether or not funding for a position will, in fact, materialize. This should not usually be a problem if a retired instructor is being replaced because the funds are already earmarked.

Politics and Competition at Your Institution. This would pertain more in colleges with large departments where some conflict is more likely.

Your Personal Background and Assets. Your own background, training, specializations, and achievements will also affect your success in the job market. Successful coursework, professional activities, and research and teaching experience will bode well, regardless of the strength of the economy (Kronenfeld & Whicker, 1997).

As a community college teacher you will learn to be a teacher, counselor, confidante, friend, guide, coach, disciplinarian, motivator, and parent. What a great opportunity to grow the next generation of thinkers and doers!

I see students dropped off at the front door by a parent and then picked up later. This is fine, but make sure the student has "bought into" education. When we discuss motivation in class, I teach students that unless they "internalize," or see the value of an education for themselves, that no prodding from parents will get that degree. External motivation is only short-term motivation.

A case in point, I had grandiose plans after high school of going into the military and then having enough money to go to college when I was discharged from the service. My parents were not rich, I wanted to go to college and I felt that would be the best solution. After many arguments with my parents that they did not want both of their boys going to Vietnam (my older brother was already in the military), I agreed to attend college for one year and then the decision would be mine with no further interference from my parents. I attended Texas Tech University in Lubbock, Texas, which is 350 miles from El Paso. I figured it was a good distance because I was far enough away but not too far that I couldn't get back home on the weekends. So to continue, the first semester I was miserable. I was checking off days on the calendar and writing home that the following May I would be going in to the military. During the spring semester, something finally clicked. I had made some friends, I started enjoying classes, and actually found myself at the library doing research and studying. This was not totally out of character for me but most of the time I would rather be shooting hoops or playing tennis. It is amazing how smart parents can be!! After spring semester, I learned the value of an education. My parents knew me better than I knew myself and for that I am grateful. I got loans for the next three years to complete my bachelor's degree.

I always revert to seeing students through my frame of reference and I must constantly guard against judging through my experiences. Sometimes I need to be reminded with my own students that everyone is at a different stage of life and some people are just not ready for the rigors of college. The student can sit in class and go through the motions but if they are not really sold on getting an education then no one can do anything to push them. I seem to want it for them more than they want it for themselves. It has been tough for me to accept and it may sound harsh, but a student has a right to fail. The best we can do is present alternatives, let them mature a bit, and then hope that they will find a positive direction for life. I always love to see former students who dropped out a few years ago return, because they are ready to learn and settle in to the idea of getting an education.

I will never forget my management professor announcing to our class that we were not there for the football team and if we were, then to drop the course. He said we were there to learn business management. I remembered after class all of us thought he was a joke and totally out of touch. That is certainly not what a college junior wants to hear! Of course, he was right, but we didn't want to admit it out loud. He soon became my mentor and I called him for advice while working on my doctorate.

As community colleges continue to grow and prosper, they will be asked by society—and by some enlightened political leaders—to do more; to help solve more problems of society, and to make up for the deficiencies of other agencies—particularly the failures of our school system. It may be that America will be creating a "new" community college that is broader in mission, more comprehensive in programming and more open to more people and to more segments of the society. In particular, they will serve the disadvantaged, minorities, urban and rural residents, and senior citizens who will live longer with greater need of intellectual stimulation.

Middle class America is now discovering the community college. Parents now are more comfortable sending their children to the hometown community college and then helping them continue their studies at the four-year college or university—even through graduate work. The stigma of attending an open admissions institution is losing its sting, making it more comfortable for high school graduates to select a community college as their choice (Smith, 1995).

Writing this has been a joy because I hope that I helped you decide if community college teaching is for you. I also hope I didn't scare you with some of my experiences, but my goal was to paint a realistic picture of teaching. I can't think of many days when I don't look forward to seeing students and challenging them to learn. Best wishes!

I'd love to continue our discussion but I need to get ready for class.

REFERENCES

Adelman, C. (2005). Moving into town--and moving on: The community college in the lives of traditional-age students. Washington, DC: U.S. Department of Education.

Alfred, R. & Carter, P. (1996). Inside track to the future. Community College Journal, 66(4), 10-19.

Alfred, R., Shults, C., Jaquette, O., & Strickland S. (2009). Community Colleges on the Horizon. New York: Rowman & Littlefield Publishing.

Anderson, L.E. & Bolt, S.B. (2013). Professionalism. San Francisco: Pearson.

Arendale, D.R. (2010). Access at the Crossroads. ASHE Higher Education Report, v. 25, no. 6.

Ayers, D. (2005). Neoliberal ideology in community college mission statements: A critical discourse analysis. The Review of Higher Education, 28 (4), 527-49.

Bailey, T., Kienzl, G., & Marcotte D. (2004). Who benefits from postsecondary occupational education? CCRC Brief no. 23. New York: Teachers College, Columbia University.

Baiocco, S.A. & DeWaters, J.N. (1998). Successful College Teaching. Boston: Allyn and Bacon.

Balli, S.J. (1999). Making a Difference in the Classroom. Lanham, MD: Rowman & Littlefield Publishing.

Bellah, R.N., et al. (2008). Habits of the Heart. Los Angeles: University of California Press.

Biggs, J. (1999). Teaching for Quality Learning at University. Buckingham: SRHE/Open University Press.

Blocker, C., Plummer, R., & Richardson, R. (1965). The Two-Year College: A Social Synthesis. Englewood Cliffs, NJ: Prentice-Hall.

Boettcher, J.V. & Conrad, R-M. (2010). The Online Teaching Survival Guide. San Francisco: Jossey-Bass.

Bourne, J. & Moore, J.C. (2003). Elements of Quality Online Education: Practice and Direction. Needham, MA: Sloan Center for Online Education at Olin and Babson Colleges.

Boylan, H.R. (2002). What works: Research-based best practices in developmental education. Boone, NC: Continuous Quality Improvement Network with the National Center for Developmental Education.

Boylan, H.R., Bonham, B.S., & Bliss, L.B. (1994). Who are the developmental students? Research in Developmental Education, 11 (2), 1-4.

Braxton, J.M., Bayer, A.E., & Noseworthy, J.A. (2004). The influence of teaching norm violations on the welfare of students as clients of college teaching. New Directions for Teaching and Learning, no. 99, 41-46. San Francisco: Jossey-Bass.

Brint, S. & Karabel, J. (1989). The Diverted Dream: Community Colleges and the Promise of Educational Opportunity in America, 1900-1985. New York: Oxford University Press.

Brookfield, S.D. (2006). The Skillful Teacher. San Francisco: Jossey-Bass.

Buttner, E.H. (2004). How do we 'dis'students? A model of (dis)respectful business instructor behavior. Journal of Management Education, 28 (3), 319-334.

Cataldi, E., Fahimi, M., & Bradburn, E.M. (2005). 2004 National Study of Postsecondary Faculty (NSOPF: 04): Report on Faculty and Instructional Staff in Fall 2003. Washington, DC: U.S. Department of Education, Office of Educational Research and Improvement.

Clement, M.C. (2010). First Time in the College Classroom. New York: Rowman & Littlefield Publishing.

Cohen, A.M. & Brawer, F.B. (1996). The American Community College. San Francisco: Jossey-Bass.

Cohen, A.M. & Brawer, F.B. (2003). The American Community College. San Francisco: Jossey-Bass.

Cox, S. & Heames, R. (1999). Managing the Pressure in Teaching. London: Falmer Press.

Craft, A. (1996). Professional Development. Milton Keynes: Open University Press.

Culp, M.M. (1998). Our present, your future. In M.M. Culp and S.R. Helfgot (Eds.), Life at the Edge of the Wave. Washington, DC: National Association of Student Personnel Administrators, Inc.

Deiner, T. (1986). Growth of an American Invention: A Documentary History of the Junior and Community College Movement. New York: Greenwood Press.

Dominowski, R.L. (2002). Teaching Undergraduates. Mahwah, NJ: Lawrence Erlbaum Associates Publishers.

Ebert, R.J. & Griffin, R.W. (2013). Business Essentials. New York: Pearson.

Eddy, P.L. (2010). New faculty issues: Fitting in and figuring it out. In B.J. Cejda & J.P. Murray (Eds.), New Directions for Community Colleges, no. 152, Winter, 15-24.

Edwards, C.H. (2000). Grade inflation: The effects on educational quality and personal well being. Education, 120, 538-547.

Floyd, C.E. (2007). Know your competitor: Impact of for-profit colleges on the higher education landscape. In L. Lapovsky & D. Klinger (Eds.), New Directions for Higher Education, no. 140, Winter, 121-128. San Francisco: Jossey-Bass.

Fowler, F.C. (2000). Policy Studies for Educational Leaders: An Introduction. Upper Saddle River, NJ: Merrill.

Fugate, A.L. & Amey, M.J. (2000). Career stages of community faculty: A qualitative analysis of their career paths, roles, and development. Community College Review, 28 (1), 1-22.

Gallant, T.B. (2008). Academic Integrity in the Twenty -First Century: A Teaching and Learning Imperative. ASHE Higher Education Report, v33, no. 5.

Gappa, J.M., Austin, A.E., &Trice, A.G. (2007). Rethinking-Faculty Work. San Francisco: Jossey-Bass.

Garner, R. (2005). Humor, analogy, and metaphor: H.A.M. it up in teaching. Radical Pedagogy, 6 (2), 1.

Ginott, H. (1972). Teacher and child: A book for parents and teachers. New York: Avon Books.

Hamm, R. (2004). Going to college: Not what it used to be. In K. Boswell & C.D. Wilson (Eds.), Keeping America's Promise. Denver, CO: Education Commission of the States.

Hammons, J. (1984). The department/division chairperson: Educational leader? Community and Junior College Journal, 54 (3), 3-7.

Hanson, C. (2010). The Community College and the Good Society. New Brunswick, NJ: Transaction Publishers.

Hargis, C.H. (2004). Grades and Grading Practices: Obstacles to Improving Education and to Helping At-Risk Students. Springfield, IL: Charles Thomas Publisher.

Harp, S. & Maslich, A. (2005). The consequences of including seductive details during lecture. Teaching of Psychology, 32 (2), 100-103.

Huberman, M. (1993). The Lives of Teachers. New York: Teachers College Press.

Kelley, W. & Wilbur, L. (1970). Teaching in the Community Junior College. New York: Meredith Corporation.

Kelly, D.K. (1990, May 2). Reviving the deadwood: How to create an institutional climate to encourage the professional growth and revitalization of mid-career faculty. Retrieved July 10, 2006, from http://www.tme21rn.com/index_files/Reviving%20the%20Deadwood.doc.

Kohn, A. (1992). No contest: The Case Against Competition. Boston: Houghton Mifflin.

Kronenfeld, J.J. & Whicker, M.L. (1997). Getting An Academic Job. Thousand Oaks, CA: Sage Publications.

Levin, J.S. & Montero-Hernandez, V. (2009). Community Colleges and Their Students. New York: Palgrave MacMillan Publishing.

Levinson, D.L. (2003). Introduction to faculty scholarship in community colleges. Community College Journal of Research and Practice, 19, no. 7, August.

Levinson, D.L. (2005). Community Colleges. Denver, CO: ABC-CLIO, Inc.

Light, G. (2000). Lifelong learning: Challenging learning and teaching in higher education. In A. Hodgson (Ed.), Policies, Politics and the Future of Lifelong Learning. London: Kogan Page.

Light, G., Cox, R., & Calkins, S. (2009). Learning and Teaching in Higher Education. Los Angeles, CA: Sage Publications.

MacIntyre, A. (1981). After Virtue. South Bend, IN: University of Notre Dame Press.

McGrath, D. & Spear, M.B. (1994). The new professoriate of community colleges. In J.L. Ratcliff (Ed.), Community Colleges. ASHE Reader Series: Simon & Schuster.

McGregor, D. (1960). The Human Side of Enterprise. New York: McGraw-Hill.

McKeachie, W.J., Pintrich, P.R., Lin, Y.G., & Smith, D.A.F. (1986). Teaching and learning in the classroom: A review of the research literature. Ann Arbor: Regents of the University of Michigan.

McKeown, M., et al. (1992). How knowledge influenced two interventions designed to improve condition. Reading Psychology, 14 (2), 141-163.

Middaugh, M.F. (2007). Creating a culture of evidence: Academic accountability at the institutional level. In L. Lapovsky & D. Klinger (Eds.), New Directions for Higher Education, no. 140, Winter, 15-28. San Francisco: Jossey-Bass.

Moallem, M. (2005). Designing and managing student assessment in an online learning environment. In P. Comeaux (Ed.), Assessing Online Learning, 18-33. San Francisco: Jossey-Bass/Anker.

Murray, J. (2001). Faculty development in publicly supported 2-year college faculty's intent to leave: An empirical model. Community College Journal of Research and Practice, 25, 487-502.

National Center for Education Statistics. (2003). Remedial education at degree-granting post-secondary institutions in Fall 2000. Washington, DC: U.S. Department of Education. Retrieved from http://nces.ed.gov/pubs2004/2004010.pdf.

National Center for Educational Statistics. (2007). The Condition of Education. Washington, DC: U.S. Department of Education.

NCES (National Center for Education Statistics). (2002). Digest of Education Statistics 2001. Washington, DC: U.S. Department of Education.

Nevarez, C. & Wood, J.L. (2010). Community College Leadership and Administration. New York: Peter Lang Publishing, Inc.

New Virginia college location. (2012, May 13). Lubbock Avalanche-Journal, E1.

Nicholls, G. (2002). Developing Teaching and Learning in Higher Education. Cambridge: University Press.

Oblinger, D. (2003). Boomers, gen-xers, and the millennials: Understanding the new students. Educause, July/August, 37-47.

Palmer, J.C. (1994). The scholarly activities of community college faculty: Findings of a national survey. In J.L. Ratcliff (Ed.), Community Colleges. ASHE Reader Series: Simon & Schuster.

Parsad, B. & Glover, D. (2002). Tenure status of postsecondary instructional faculty and staff: 1992-1998. Washington, DC: National Center for Educational Statistics.

Phelps, P.H. & Benson, T.R. (2012). Teachers with a passion for the profession. Action in Teacher Education, v34, no. 1, 65-76.

Phillippe, K.A. & Sullivan, L.G. (2005). National Profile of Community Colleges: Trends & Statistics. Washington, DC: American Association of Community Colleges, Community College Press.

Pollak, J.P. & Freda, P.D. (1997). Humor, learning, and socialization in middle level classrooms. The Clearing House, 70, 176-178.

Portolan, J.S. (1992). Developing statewide organization and exploring a redefined role for instructional administrators in California community colleges. Unpublished doctoral dissertation. University of California, Los Angeles.

Pullias, E.V., Lockhart, A., et al. (1963). Toward Excellence in College Teaching. Dubuque, IA: Wm. C. Brown.

Quintilian. (1969). Institutio Oratoria of Quintilian. English translation by H.E. Butler. Cambridge, MA: Harvard University Press.

Reece, B.L. Brandt, R., & Howie, K.F. (2011). Effective Human Relations. Mason, OH: South-Western, Cengage Learning.

Rodriguez, R.C. (2010). Legal concerns in community college employment matters. In B.D. Cejda & J.P. Murray (Eds.). New Directions for Community Colleges, no. 152, Winter, 57-69.

Rosenbaum, J.E., Deil-Amen, R., & Person, A.E. (2006). After Admission. New York: Russell Sage Foundation.

Rosser, V.J. & Townsend, B.K. (2006). Determining public 2-year college faculty's intent to leave: An empirical model. Journal of Higher Education, 77 (1), 124-147.

Ruskin, J. (1851). Pre-Raphaelitism. London: Smith Elder and Co.

Schmid, C. (2010). Challenges and opportunities of community colleges. In F. Lazin, M. Evans, & N. Jayarams (Eds.), Higher Education and Equality of Opportunities. Boulder, CO: Rowman & Littlefield Publishers, Inc.

Scott, C. (2010). Vocatio: The importance of exploring an ancient concept for community college students. In K. Kroll (Ed.). New Directions for Community Colleges, no. 151, Fall, 101-110.

Sewell, W., Haller, A., & Portes, A. (1969). The educational and early occupational attainment process. American Sociological Review, 34, 82-92.

Smith, R.W. (1995). Tomorrow's Community College. Princeton Academic Press: Life Press, Inc.

Tierney, W.G. & Hentschke, G.C. (2007). New Players, Different Game. Baltimore: The John Hopkins University Press.

Townley, C. & Parsell, M. (2004). Technology and academic virtue: Student plagiarism through the looking glass. Ethics and Information Technology, 6, 271-277.

Townsend, B.K. & Twombly, S.B. (2007). Community College Faculty: Overlooked and Undervalued. ASHE-ERIC Higher Education Report, No. 32-6, Hoboken, NJ: Wiley.

U.S. Census Bureau (2008). Current population survey, 2008 annual social and economic supplement.

VanDerLinden, K. (2002). Credit student analysis: 1999 and 2000. Washington, DC: American Association of Community Colleges, and Ames, IA: ACT, Inc.

Vaughn, G.B. (2000). The Community College Story. Washington, DC: Community College Press.

Waits, T. & Lewis, L. (2003). Distance Education at Degree-Granting Postsecondary Institutions: 2001-01. NCES 2003-17. Washington, DC: U.S. Department of Education, National Center for Education Statistics.

Walvoord, B.F. & Anderson, V.J. (1998). Effective Grading. San Francisco: Jossey-Bass. Webster's Ninth New College Dictionary. (1991). Springfield, MA: Merriam-Webster, Inc.

Wieman, C. (2008). Science education in the 21st century: Using the tools of science to teach science. Forum features 2008.EDUCAUSE. Retrieved November 3, 2008, from http://net.educause.edu/ir/library/pdf/ff0814s.pdf.

Wilhelm, J.D. (1996). Teacher effectiveness in a community college: Student and teacher perceptions. (Doctoral Dissertation). Texas Tech University, Lubbock, TX.

Wilson, C. (2004). Coming through the open door: A student profile. In K. Boswell & C.D. Wilson (Eds.), Keeping America's Promise. Denver, CO: Education Commission of the States, pp. 25-27.

Winner, C.N. (1989). The role and function of the departmental chairperson at Delaware Technical and Community College. Three position papers submitted as Ed.D. requirements, University of Delaware.

Zaslow, J. (2006, February 16). First impressions get faster. The Wall Street Journal, D4.

APPENDIX
Survey

Are You College Teacher material?

Take this survey as an indicator of whether you have what it takes. Please answer the following questions:

Circle "Yes" or "No"

1. Are you a team player?
    Yes   No
2. Do you consider yourself a multi-tasker?
    Yes   No
3. Have you achieved most of your goals?
    Yes   No
4. Do you enjoy helping others?
    Yes   No
5. Do you work better with a routine?
    Yes   No
6. Do you see your commitments through?
    Yes   No
7. Are you competitive?
    Yes   No
8. Do you have a lot of patience?
    Yes   No
9. Are you a good role model?
    Yes   No
10. Do you enjoy applying theories?
    Yes   No
11. Do you like socializing with coworkers?
    Yes   No
12. Do you enjoy learning new things?
    Yes   No
13. Do you prefer to lead rather than follow?
    Yes   No
14. Do you understand your limits and not stretching yourself too thin?
    Yes   No

15. Do you believe you should give back?
    Yes   No
16. Do you question things?
    Yes   No
17. Would you make up an answer if you weren't sure?
    Yes   No
18. Can you empathize and see someone else's point of view?
    Yes   No
19. Are you an organized person?
    Yes   No
20. In a disagreement, do you search for a solution/compromise?
    Yes   No
21. Do you believe everyone in the U.S. should go to college?
    Yes   No
22. Do you have ways to relieve stress?
    Yes   No
23. Do you enjoy meetings?
    Yes   No
24. Do you have a sense of humor?
    Yes   No
25. Would you quit if you've had no raise in 3 years?
    Yes   No
26. Are you a punctual person?
    Yes   No
27. If you know you're right in a disagreement, do you
    continue pushing your agenda?
    Yes   No
28. Do you enjoy working flexible hours?
    Yes   No
29. Do you get excited about things?
    Yes   No
30. Do you have a lot of self-discipline?
    Yes   No

Scoring: Score only the even-numbered questions and give yourself 10 points for every "yes" answer.

Scoring Summary
120-150 – Welcome to community college teaching! You will impact many students' lives positively. Have a great career!

90-110 – If you set your mind to it, you can be an effective community college teacher. You have the potential, but you must develop it.

60-80 – Probably not a wise career choice.

50 or less – Please, keep away from the students!

Answer explanations:
1.   Are you a team player? This is not crucial to success in the classroom, but it certainly helps with colleagues and activities outside the classroom and, of course, employment in general.
2.   **Do you consider yourself a multi-tasker? This is crucial**. You will be preparing for class, counseling students, working on budgets, dealing with colleagues, going to meetings. If you are not a multi-tasker it will be hard to succeed at this job.
3.   Have you achieved most of your goals? It would be helpful, but I don't see this as a reflection of whether you can be a successful college teacher.
4.   **Do you enjoy helping others? This is crucial**. If you do not enjoy helping others, then teaching is probably not for you.
5.   Do you work better with a routine? I do not think this is a barometer of successful teaching. There are great teachers who have no routine at all. It comes down to being committed to students and doing a good job of preparation whether you are in a routine or not.
6.   **Do you see your commitments through? This is crucial**. This has a bearing on class preparation, exams, deadlines, and so forth. If you start a lot of projects and never complete them, it will not bode well for teaching.

7.   Are you competitive? No real bearing on teaching success.
Sometimes competitiveness gives way to jealousies. You are your
own person and if you use competition to motivate you quietly then
it may assist in helping you achieve goals.

8.   **Do you have a lot of patience? This is crucial**. There will
be days when you are totally flustered with other things and then you
have to head into the classroom. Patience is the key to teaching.
Your patience will be tried and tried again. Have plenty of patience.

9.   Are you a good role model? This is important. Students
look to you for guidance so be a good role model. Do you dress and
act professionally? Do you listen to questions?

10.   **Do you enjoy applying theories? This is important**. You
will be not only explaining theories but also applying them so
students can understand and use them.

11.   Do you enjoy socializing with coworkers? Not crucial, but
certainly helpful. There will be get togethers and if you like
socializing with coworkers, it makes it easier. You do not want to be
the "weird one," who always keeps to themselves. As in any
employment, liking your coworkers is a big part of the liking the job.

12.   **Do you enjoy learning new things? This is crucial**. You
will learn not only from your own research and textbooks but from
students as well. We need to constantly keep the mind open for
learning.

13.   Do you prefer to lead rather than follow? This really does
not matter. You probably will not be pushed into a leadership
position if you don't strive for that. We need both leaders and
followers.

14.   **Do you understand your limits and not stretching
yourself too thin? This is crucial**. You will learn how many
different courses you can teach effectively and what your limits are.
Try to never go beyond that. I am comfortable with having four
preparations and this semester I have five. I like to think I can
handle it, but in reality, it is a bit too much and the only one who
suffers is students.

15.   Do you believe you should give back? Again, it is great to
feel that way, and I hope you do, but it is not crucial to being a good
teacher.

16.   **Do you question things? This is an important quality.** It means that you are on the cutting edge of teaching and hopefully bringing new ideas into the classroom.

17.   Would you make up an answer if you weren't sure? A teacher should never give less than accurate information because students look to us for the necessary information. I didn't consider this as crucial because if the student finds out you gave out erroneous information, it will be embarrassing enough for you.

18.   **Can you empathize and see another's point of view? This is an important quality.** This helps meet student needs and increases teaching effectiveness.

19.   Are you an organized person? It helps, but not crucial to success. (Please don't look at my office) A certain amount of organization is probably necessary to get the job done well.

20.   **In a disagreement, do you search for a solution or a compromise? This is crucial.** There will be disagreement in the classroom and how you handle it will reflect on your teaching style. I have always felt a teacher can impose their will on the class but it does not make for a friendly learning atmosphere.

21.   Do you believe everyone in the U.S. should go to college? This has no bearing on teaching.

22.   **Do you have ways to relieve stress? This is crucial in any job.** Please find an outlet for your frustrations. It makes one healthier in the long run.

23.   Do you enjoy meetings? This is not crucial, but since you have to attend you might as well grow to enjoy, or at least tolerate, them.

24.   **Do you have a sense of humor? This is crucial.** If you can laugh rather than cry, that is a virtue! I think this question pared with the stress release question is so important. Don't take things too seriously because we all make mistakes, just laugh and go on.

25.   Would you quit if you've had no raise in 3 years? There is no bearing on your teaching with this question, but it could become reality. With state budget cuts you would have to make that decision and what financial shape you are in.

26.   **Are you a punctual person? This is crucial.** You must be on time for class and that carries over to meeting times, appointments with students and so on. It really comes down to

commitment. If you are committed to your job then you will be on time.

27. If you know you're right in a disagreement, do you continue pushing your agenda? This relates back to teaching style. There will be many disagreements in class and you can impose your will but a better way might to look at all sides and lead the students to the right conclusion.

28. **Do you enjoy working flexible hours? This is crucial**. You will be shifting class hours occasionally to meet student needs. You must learn to adjust to teaching, morning, and/or evening classes as demand dictates. It is the only way to reach the most students.

29. Do you get excited about things? This is nice, but not necessary. It does show enthusiasm, but you can be an effective teacher without getting excited.

30. **Do you have a lot of self-discipline? This is crucial**. This is a large part of teaching. You need self-discipline to keep office hours, you need self-discipline to prepare and be on time for class, and you need self-discipline to get papers graded in a timely manner to give students feedback. No one will be looking over your shoulder to make sure you get things done so self-discipline is huge when it comes to teaching.

Made in the USA
Monee, IL
05 March 2022